THE AFFORDABLE HOUSING CRISIS:

Causes and Cures

Brian Phillips

TABLE OF CONTENTS

PART 1

The Thinking that Caused the Housing Crisis

*We fail more often because we solve the wrong
problem than because we get
the wrong solution to the right problem.* Russell L. Ackoff

Few people deny that America has a severe shortage of affordable housing for low- and moderate-income households. While there is agreement that a problem exists, there is little agreement about a remedy. Government officials at every level, along with housing advocates, frequently put forth a variety of policy proposals in an attempt to address the problem.

For more than a century, government officials have created an assortment of programs and policies in an attempt to provide Americans with safe, decent, and affordable housing. The fact that today the affordable housing problem is worse than ever is testament that these programs and policies have failed. Despite this failure, we are routinely subjected to new policy proposals that are simply a variation on the same theme.

The reason for this continued failure is the framework that has been employed since the beginning of the twentieth century. That manner of thinking led to numerous policies that exacerbated a modest housing problem. And the continued application of that framework has steadily made the problem worse.

The affordability of housing is determined by many factors, not just the price for rent or a mortgage. For example, monetary policies have a direct impact on the interest rates charged for mortgages and new construction. Laws such as occupational licensing stifle the ability of individuals to start a business or enter a profession—i.e., improve one's income. The impact on the affordability of housing of these and other policies must be identified and considered. Unfortunately, the same flawed framework that has been guiding housing policy has also been guiding policies in other areas.

If we truly want to solve the affordable housing crisis, then we must reject the thinking method that has dominated discussions of housing and related policies for more than a century. We must be willing to embrace a new framework, a new way of thinking about housing policy.

In Part 1, I address the thinking that caused the housing crisis and continues to make it worse. We will examine the dominant framework, as well as an alternative. In Part 2, I look at the housing policies (and related policies) that were developed in the late 1800s and early 1900s. We will see how these policies impact the affordability of housing. In Part 3, I examine contemporary policies pertaining to housing. We will see that contemporary policies may differ from the failed policies of the past in details, but in principle they are the same. In Part 4, I present alternatives policies to address the housing crisis. I will show how we can truly enable all Americans to have safe, decent, and affordable housing.

THE WRONG FRAMEWORK LEADS TO BAD RESULTS

In mid-March 2018, I signed a lease with a new tenant. At the time, she paid her security deposit and a pro-rated amount for the remainder of the month. A week after she moved in, she contacted me to say that the kitchen drain was clogged. I went by the house the next day and quickly removed the clog. On the last day of the month, she informed me that the kitchen sink was clogged again, and so was the bathtub. I arranged to meet her the next day, but that morning she texted to reschedule. Two days later, I unclogged the kitchen sink again but was unable to do so with the bathtub. I told her that I would contact my plumber.

Before I left, I asked her about the rent for April. She said that she would get a money order later in the day and make arrangements to meet me on her way out of town for the weekend. She didn't contact me until Monday after she returned from her trip. When she did call, she immediately started screaming at me that I hadn't fixed the tub. I reminded her that she had been out of town and couldn't have given the plumber access. "My sister could have met him," she yelled. "You need to do your f...... job."

When I asked about the rent and pointed out that she hadn't contacted me as she had promised, she informed me that she wasn't going to pay anything until the clog was removed.

My plumber contacted her later that day to arrange a visit to the house. The tenant told him that she wasn't available until three days later. When my plumber arrived at the appointed time, she informed him that she had an emergency to deal with. Apparently, her sister could no longer provide access. The plumber was busy for the next few days, so I contacted another plumber. My backup plumber met with the tenant the following day and quickly unclogged the tub.

In the process of removing the clog, the plumber discovered that the main drain was broken. While it was still functional, it was likely that within a few months the cast iron pipe would completely collapse, and the drain would be inoperable. He gave me a price that was more than twice what I had previously paid for similar work. I told him that I needed to talk with my partner, and I wanted to get another estimate. Since the drain was working, I didn't regard this as an issue requiring immediate action, and it wasn't. There was no threat to the tenant's health or safety.

By this point, it was well into April and the tenant had still not paid that month's rent. When I met with her to discuss the situation, she announced that she wouldn't pay the rent until we replaced the broken drain, even though everything in the house drained properly.

I explained that I wanted to get more estimates for the work since it wasn't an emergency. "But tell me," I asked, "how do you expect me to pay for repairs if you aren't paying the rent?"

"That's your problem," she replied. "My sister is a realtor and I know my rights. This house is unlivable and has been since the day I moved in. The drains have been clogged since day one."

"You didn't say anything for a week, and I fixed that the very next day. I can't fix something if I'm not aware that it's broken," I said. "All of the clogs have been removed. You need to pay the rent."

"You lied to me," she shouted. "You told me that this house has never flooded. But the house down the street flooded last week and I see a rotted board outside."

I chuckled. "This house didn't flood last week, so what happened down the street is irrelevant. In the eight years I have owned the house, it hasn't flooded. And that includes Harvey (a hurricane that dumped more than 50 inches of rain on Houston over four days). If it flooded before I owned it, I am unaware of that fact."

"Well, I'm still not paying until you fix the drain," she said. "That is the only way you can resolve this."

I shook my head. "No, there is another way to resolve this. I can evict you."

"You can't evict me. I know my rights. My sister is a realtor," she repeated.

Three weeks later, we met in court. The judge asked her if she had paid the rent. "No. But I paid him a lot of money to move in and…."

The judge interrupted her. "Let me offer you some advice young lady. If you want to make the rules, buy your own property. Judgment for the plaintiff." Obviously upset over the turn of events, the tenant stormed from the courtroom without a word.

My tenant's experience obviously did not end well for her. She did not achieve the results she desired. The conclusion to this conflict was not a result of a system that favors landlords over tenants. The conclusion was the result of my tenant's thinking method. The wrong framework leads to bad results.

Our framework defines how we will analyze and evaluate anything that requires a decision—a policy proposal, an idea, or a problem. It defines, not only how we will evaluate the facts, but also which facts we will consider. If we want to make good decisions about what course of action to take, then we must embrace a method of thinking that will allow us to objectively evaluate a problem and alternative solutions.

My tenant did not do this, and the result was undesirable for her. If she had embraced the proper framework, the issue could have been resolved to our mutual benefit. So, what was wrong with the tenant's method of thinking about the issue?

She began with the wrong objective. She was trying to solve the wrong problem, and thus her efforts ended in failure. She wanted a house that was devoid of any defects. Her objective was unreasonable, and it could be argued that it was impossible. Regardless, the broken drain had no impact on her health or safety, nor did it prevent her from living normally. If I had not told her about the drain being broken, she wouldn't have even known about it. Yet, because her standard required a "perfect" house, she was unwilling to accommodate anything short of perfection. Her subsequent actions were guided by this unreasonable objective.

Because I was not meeting her goal, she refused to pay the rent. While the Texas Property Code allows tenants to withhold rent because repairs have not been made, a tenant must follow a specific procedure. That procedure includes providing notification in writing of the needed repairs (and those repairs must pertain to a threat to health or safety) and allowing the property owner a "reasonable" amount of time to remedy the problem. My tenant did neither of these.

The wrong objective was only the starting point. Nearly everything that the tenant did after I told her about the broken drain was guided by her flawed goal. My tenant's objective determined what facts she would consider and how she would evaluate those facts.

Each time I met with the tenant, she would hurl accusations and claims at me. She insisted that the house had flooded and claimed that I was aware of that fact. Her evidence was the presence of wood decay on one exterior board. When I pointed out that wood is prone to rot in Houston's climate even when it doesn't flood, she then told me that a house down the street had recently flooded. When I pointed out that her house was about four feet higher from the road than the house down the street, she complained about flies in the house when she moved in. When I suggested that they might have gotten in while she was moving, she complained that the broken drain would cause her to have a high water bill. When I explained that her water bill is based on what comes out of the faucet, and the broken drain had no impact on that, she then told me how bad her previous landlord had been.

In short, each statement I made was quickly dismissed. She didn't address any of my points. Instead, she simply made another claim or accusation and changed the subject. The connection between her statements was impossible to determine, other than they were somehow "evidence" of my negligence. The tenant's disintegrated, rambling approach was a result of her objective.

The facts are not on the side of the person who begins with an unreasonable goal. That person must invent "facts," ignore actual facts, or both. In place of actual facts, my tenant said anything that she believed would help achieve her objective, even if those statements weren't true or relevant. My tenant was deluding herself and hoping to delude me. But her wishes did not change the facts. And this is an example of the second flaw in her framework.

The tenant evaluated every statement that I made through the lens of her objective. Anything that did not support her goal was to be dismissed. She was unable to consider any fact that did not comport with her objective. She was unable to consider the full context.

The full context means all of the relevant facts. If my tenant had looked at all of the facts, she would have realized that I had made a conscientious effort to fix the problem and it was her schedule that delayed a remedy to the clog. If she had considered the full context, she would have realized that the drain was functional and would be repaired soon. If she had looked at all of the facts, she would have understood that the house down the street that had flooded was at a much lower elevation, and thus, more likely to flood than the house in which she was living. If she had considered the full context, she would have taken a different course of action and had a much better result. But she didn't consider all of the relevant facts, and the results speak for themselves.

One consequence of dropping context—not considering the full context—is a myopic view of an issue or idea. If we drop context, then we ignore anything that is not immediately and obviously related to what we are considering. We willfully put blinders on, preventing ourselves from considering facts that might give us a different perspective and lead to different conclusions.

In the case of my tenant, she wanted the broken drain repaired immediately. The reasons why I refused an immediate repair were deemed irrelevant by her. To her, nothing else mattered. Until the drain was repaired, I was in the wrong. In dropping context, my tenant was unable to consider alternatives, which was the final flaw in her framework.

My tenant observed some fact and then drew conclusions, many of which were wildly inaccurate. For example, when I offered an alternative explanation regarding the nearby house that had flooded, my statement was summarily dismissed, not worth any consideration. The same occurred each time I offered an alternative explanation regarding flies in the house, the presence of wood rot, a creaking floor board, or anything else. In her mind, the only alternative worth considering was that I was being negligent.

Nor did she consider any alternative to withholding the rent. Her attitude was, "Do as I demand, or I won't pay the rent." She made no attempt to find a mutually beneficial solution.

The tenant's framework made it impossible for her to make decisions that would lead to a favorable outcome. From the starting point of choosing the wrong objective to refusing to consider the full context to dismissing alternatives, she sabotaged her ability to make the best decisions.

As the story of my tenant illustrates, when the wrong method is used to discuss and evaluate a problem or issue, it is unlikely that the best decisions will be made. Unfortunately, for more than a century, discussions about housing policy and related issues have been founded on a flawed thinking method.

The result has been a series of decisions that have not solved the problem, and have in fact, made it worse. A house cannot be built, nor good decisions made, without the proper framework. With the wrong framework guiding policy discussions since the early twentieth century, the affordable housing problem has only grown worse over the decades.

THE SEEDS OF A HOUSING CRISIS

The seeds of today's housing crisis were planted in the late nineteenth century and early twentieth century during the Progressive Era and the Great Depression. During the late nineteenth century,
many aspiring American intellectuals—such as philosophers, economists, and historians—traveled to Europe, and particularly Germany, for their graduate degrees. In Europe, they were introduced to ideas that were foreign in America. Those ideas would not remain foreign for long.

When the intellectuals returned to the United States, they began disseminating these ideas. They began framing policy discussions based on what they had learned in Europe. While the intellectuals disagreed on some details, they agreed on the fundamental issues. As their ideas became widely accepted, America began to be transformed. Initially, housing was only marginally impacted by this new framework. But by the end of World War II, housing became a central focus of the federal government.

Most of the policies that we will examine in later chapters were developed and implemented during the Progressive Era (1890-1915) or during the Great Depression (1929-1939). During this period, the Progressive framework was firmly established and it has dominated housing policy discussions in the decades since. To understand this new framework, let us begin by looking at the Progressive intellectuals.

The Progressive Intellectuals

Upon returning from Europe, the Progressive intellectuals entered nearly every field in the humanities. Their ideas were injected into the culture in myriad ways, including books, magazine and newspaper articles, speeches, and most importantly, on college campuses. In the college classrooms, professors indoctrinated a new generation of Progressive intellectuals.

Echoing their European teachers, the Progressives argued that individuals do not exist as independent beings, but only as a member of the group. Philosopher James Edwin Creighton captured the essence of this view:

> We have been forced to abandon the notion of *exclusive* individuality, and to recognize that individuals have reality and significance, not in themselves and by natural or divine right; but just in so far as they embody and express the life and purpose of a larger social whole of which they are members. It is as *members of society*, not as self-subsistent entities, that individuals must be interpreted.[1]

Individuals, according to Creighton, are merely cells in the organism that is society—the collective.

Charles R. Van Hise, the president of the University of Wisconsin, added a twist to this ethos, saying, "He who thinks not of himself primarily, but of his race, and of its future, is the new patriot."[2] In other words, the individual should not think about his own happiness, but the alleged well-being of his race— the group.

Pragmatism, the dominant philosophy of the Progressive Era, provided a philosophical justification for the new framework. One of the central tents of Pragmatism is that objective truth does not exist. William James, one of the founders of Pragmatism, wrote,

> Purely objective truth, truth in whose establishment the

function of giving human satisfaction in marrying previous parts of experience with newer parts played no role whatsoever, is nowhere to be found. The reasons why we call things true is the reason why they are true, for "to be true" means only to perform this marriage-function.[3]

For James, each individual performs this "marriage-function." Each individual determines what is true for him. The German philosopher Friedrich Nietzsche shared James's view, writing, "'*You have your* way. I *have my* way. As for *the* right way, *the* correct way, and *the* only way, it does not exist." A more colloquial way of expressing this sentiment is, "You have your truth and I have mine." While James agreed with Nietzsche, he was in the minority among Pragmatism philosophers. The dominant view was advanced by John Dewey.

Dewey agreed that there is no objective truth or objective reality. In Dewey's words, reality is "malleable," "plastic," "unfinished."[4] Unlike James and Nietzsche, Dewey held that truth is determined by the collective consciousness, not the individual. Moreover, the collective consciousness can mold and shape reality to its will. This gave rise to the Progressive's political views.

The political scientist John W. Burgess, a professor of constitutional law at what later became Columbia and founder of the *Political Science Quarterly*, which has published continuously since 1886 stated the political philosophy of Progressives, writing that

> the state is the source of individual liberty. The revolutionists of the eighteenth century said that individual liberty was natural right; that it belonged to the individual as a human being, without regard to the state or society in which, or the government under which, he lived. But it is easy to see that this view is utterly impracticable and barren; for, if neither the state nor the society defines the sphere of individual autonomy and constructs its boundaries, then the individual himself will be left to these things, and that is anarchy pure and simple.[5]

Another intellectual leader at the time, Richard Ely, was a founding member of the American Economic Association, whose constitution stated: "We regard the state as an agency whose positive assistance is one of the indispensable conditions of human progress."[6]

These intellectuals agreed that government—with input from experts—should plan, control, and regulate the activities of the citizenry. They agreed that individuals should subordinate their self-interest and values to the "common good." They claimed that the individual should not act in the pursuit of his own happiness, but in service to the "general welfare."

Building on Dewey's view that the collective consciousness molds and shapes truth and reality, the Progressives acted on the premise that if enough people wanted a policy to be beneficial, it would be. If enough people put aside their self-interest in deference to the "public interest," we could create a more perfect society. And when individuals won't do so voluntarily, then they must be forced to do so. The "greater good" demands it.

Nearly every issue or problem was evaluated through this framework. The "public interest" became the standard by which policies were evaluated.

The Progressive Framework's Standard Is The Group

The Progressive framework is wrong in every regard. It begins with an inappropriate standard, refuses to consider the full context, and regards the consideration of alternatives as impossible.

For Progressives, the standard for evaluating any policy is the alleged well-being of the group—the tribe, the community, the nation, the public. It was and remains an explicitly collectivist standard. Harvard Professor Josiah Royce was considered one of the giants of American philosophy during the Progressive Era. One of his most influential works was *The World and the Individual*, in which he gave voice to the Progressive view:

> The central evil of our life is selfishness. Virtue is definable as altruism, i.e., as forgetting ourselves in the thought of others. The best eulogy that one can make over the grave of a departed saint is: He had no thought of Self; he served; he sacrificed himself; he gave himself as an offering for the good of mankind; he lived for others; he never even observed his own virtues; he forsook himself; he asked for nothing but bondage to his duty.[7]

Herbert Croly, the founder of *The New Republic* magazine, echoed the other Progressive intellectuals, writing,

> The Promise of American Life is to be fulfilled—not merely by a maximum amount of economic freedom, but by a certain measure of discipline, not merely by the abundant satisfaction of individual desires, but by a large measure of individual subordination and self-denial.[8]

The individual, according to the Progressive intellectuals, existed, not for his own personal happiness, but to self-sacrificially serve others. The well-being of the collective, not the individual, is the standard of value. The collectivist holds that individuals do not have rights, and the group may do with him as it pleases. This ethos has been dominating discussions of housing and related policies ever since.

As an example, in the early twentieth century many cities used zoning to achieve both economic and racial segregation for the explicit purpose of protecting property values for whites. The alleged well-being of whites was used to justify legally prohibiting blacks from living in certain neighborhoods. The group—white homeowners—served as the standard. Today, zoning is used to promote and protect the values of another group—the community—when evaluating land-use policies.

As a contemporary example, housing advocates routinely

call for laws to protect "tenants' rights." They advocate a number of policies to promote this agenda, including rent control, eviction moratoriums, public defenders for eviction hearings, and more. The alleged well-being of the group—tenants—serves as the standard when evaluating policies pertaining to rental housing.

As a final example, many housing advocates focus their efforts on providing subsidies and support for low-income households. They advocate for expanding the housing voucher program and requiring developers to include below market-rate housing in their projects. The alleged well-being of the group—low-income households—serves as the standard when evaluating policies regarding affordable housing.

In each of these examples, and countless others, the collective serves as the standard. Though they may choose different groups, housing advocates and politicians on both sides of the aisle have long agreed that the alleged well-being of one group or another is the standard that should be used when evaluating policies. With this as their starting point, they then evaluate policies from the perspective of the favored group. If a policy is judged to benefit the collective, it is good and should be supported. If it won't benefit the collective, it is bad and should be opposed. This is the framework advanced by Progressives more than one hundred years ago and it still holds sway.

When collectivists talk about the good of the group, what they really mean is that the good for some individuals should take precedence over the good for other individuals. This is precisely what happens when the Progressive framework is put into practice. The alleged good of tenants must be achieved at the expense of landlords. The alleged good of low-income families must be achieved at the expense of property owners, developers, and taxpayers. This is Herbert Croly's idea of "individual subordination" in practice.

When the good for some can only be achieved at the expense of others, a power struggle naturally ensues as rival gangs seek to gain political power and influence. The collectivist seeks to control others to do his bidding. The collectivist holds that individuals should not deal with one another voluntarily, that some must be compelled to sacrifice for the group. This invariably pits members of the group against non-members of the group, such as middle- or high-income individuals against low-income households, tenants versus landlords, or the community versus gentrifying developers. Non-members of the favored group are penalized, not because of wrongdoing on their part, but simply because they are non-members. "Justice" for one group can only come at the expense of injustice for others.

When the group serves as the standard, the individual must sacrifice his values, interests, and judgment to those of the collective. When the group—any group—serves as the standard, the individual—every individual—is subservient to the collective. This is the embodiment of Josiah Royce's saint: individuals should not think of themselves; they must self-sacrificially serve others. And those who do not do so voluntarily should be compelled to do so.

There is nothing wrong with wanting to help low-income households attain affordable housing. But our focus, and our standard, should not be the group, but rather, the individual. Our standard must enable each individual to attain his goals and dreams, including affordable housing. Our standard must apply to everyone. This cannot occur when the group serves as the standard. We cannot enable the individual while subordinating him to the collective.

The Progressive Framework Drops Context

"Context" means, in the words of philosopher Leonard Peikoff, "the sum of cognitive elements conditioning an item of human knowledge."[9] Peikoff goes on to say that when the full context is not kept in awareness, claims, proposals, and issues are treated in isolation.

To illustrate, we do not communicate in isolated words. We put multiple words together to convey a thought. However, if someone quotes only select words, we can be made to appear to have said something very different from our original statement. I might write, "I think Hitler was an evil man, but some think that Hitler was a hero." If only the last four words are quoted, it appears that I admire Hitler, which is very different from my full statement. A similar distortion occurs when a policy or proposal is considered out-of-context.

When a policy or proposal is not considered in the full context—when the context is dropped—we treat it as an isolated issue, with no effects from or on other issues. As an example, when the pandemic began, governments began a course of action without considering the full context. The only concern was stopping the spread of the novel coronavirus, and so they ordered businesses to close and "non-essential" workers to stay home. The economic destruction of a lock down was not considered until it became impossible to ignore.

In the Progressive framework, considering the full context is summarily rejected. Indeed, the Progressive framework claims that predicting future consequences is impossible. We must take action and wait for the results. As the influential Progressive philosopher John Dewey put it, we must accept "the fundamental idea that we know only after we have acted and in consequence of the outcome of an action."[10] If we take Dewey seriously, and we should, we don't know that poking our eye with a sharp stick will hurt until we actually do it. This, of course, is absurd. We can know the consequences of poking our eye with a sharp stick without the need to actually do so.

Public policies are not enacted in a vacuum. They can have widespread consequences far into the future. They can, and almost always do, impact many other issues. When we consider the full context, we look beyond the immediate results and project the consequences months, years, perhaps decades from now. And we do this for all of the relevant and related issues. This is not possible, the Progressives claim. Instead, we must experiment, judge the results, and repeat this process until we finally get the desired results.

This framework demands that we look only at the moment, that we reject the notion of identifying the relationship between different issues, that we refuse to consider how a policy or action might impact those who aren't targeted for the benefits.

With this method of thinking firmly entrenched, policies are proposed, considered, and then implemented with promises of grand benefits. The promises are seldom realized, but that is acceptable because the Progressive framework holds that the consequences of an action cannot be predicted. One must act, and if the results are not acceptable, we must choose another course of action. This approach is nothing more than trial and error. We must keep experimenting until we find a policy that is successful.

The Progressive framework does more than explicitly reject consideration of the full context. It demands that one drop context.

Dropping context necessarily involves looking at facts and issues in isolation. As an example, defenders of single-family zoning argue that land-use regulations are necessary to protect property values. They make no mention of the fact that single-family zoning arbitrarily restricts the supply of land for housing, thereby driving up the price of housing. These defenders refuse to consider other related issues.

As another example of dropping context, many tenants and housing advocates loudly proclaim that "the rent is too damn high." To illustrate this point, one housing advocate wrote, "In 2019, Zillow recently reported, Los Angeles renters paid landlords a whopping $39.1 billion. In San Francisco and San Diego, renters shelled out $16.4 billion and $10.3 billion, respectively, to landlords. It's no wonder that California's housing affordability and homelessness crises haven't improved."[11]

The author implies that those numbers explain the high cost of housing. But the amounts paid for rent are only a small part of the context. There are many other factors that are a part of the context if we are going to evaluate the affordability of housing, and the failure to identify and consider all of them can lead to erroneous conclusions. As a small part of the full context, in 2019 the median rent in Los Angeles County was $1,577[12] and the median income was $68,000[13]. In Los Angeles, a renter making the median income and paying the median rent spent 28 percent of his income on housing in 2019. The median rent in San Francisco was $2,057 in 2019[14] and the median household income was $123,589[15]. A renter paying the median rent and making the median income would pay less than 20 percent in 2019. In both Los Angeles and San Francisco, these medians are within the range that is considered affordable and presents a much different picture than the numbers presented by the housing advocate.

Granted, these numbers are medians, and they tell us nothing about specific individuals. They do not provide the full context, but they are an important part of the context. The point here is that when context is dropped the conclusions that we reach will be misleading. The full context matters, and if we want to make wise choices, then we must continually consider the full context. The Progressive framework rejects such considerations. At the same time, that framework makes it impossible to consider the pros and cons of alternatives.

The Progressive Framework Ignores The Pros And Cons Of Alternative Policies

According to the Progressives, we can't know the results of an action until we have acted. If we cannot project the future consequences of today's actions, then we have no means by which to evaluate the pros and cons of alternative policies. We cannot say that one policy will have good results and another policy won't. All we can do is implement a policy and evaluate the results after the fact. The Progressive framework disables the means by which we can evaluate a policy and its alternatives objectively. And if we cannot evaluate alternatives objectively, it is impossible to choose the best policy.

As an example of this point, in the early 1990s, Houston government officials began developing plans to bring zoning to the nation's fourth largest city. When I and other opponents of zoning pointed to the problems caused by zoning in other cities, pro-zoners argued that what has happened in Detroit, Miami, New York City, and other cities with zoning is irrelevant. Those cities aren't Houston, and until we have zoning, nobody can predict what will happen in Houston.

Zoning advocates vehemently rejected any claim that zoning would create problems in Houston, calling such suggestions lies and misrepresentations. Because they embraced the Progressive framework, zoning advocates believed that opponents could not predict the results of zoning. Any attempt to do so was deceitful. Fortunately, enough Houstonians rejected the Progressive argument, and the zoning plan was defeated in a 1993 referendum.

This story illustrates the myopic perspective imposed by the Progressive framework. The pro-zoners made grand promises regarding the benefits that zoning would bring to Houston, and then they simply refused to acknowledge any problems that zoning might cause. They looked only at the pros of their proposal and ignored any cons. They refused to acknowledge any of the pros of a more laissez faire approach to land use. Because of their framework, zoning advocates were unable to examine the issue objectively.

This is repeated time and again. Progressives introduce a policy proposal and tout its many alleged benefits without a word of any negative consequences. For example, rent control advocates argue that capping rents will benefit tenants, which is true in the short-term. However, it is widely acknowledged that rent control degrades both the quantity and the quality of rental housing in the long-term. Rent control advocates seldom address this fact. They look only at what is immediately beneficial and ignore the long-term harm.

As another example, when the pandemic began and governments started shutting down businesses, the results were easy to predict. Many people would lose their job and be unable to pay their rent or mortgage. The policy makers looked only at the immediate problem—stopping the spread of the coronavirus. They chose to act without considering the long-term consequences. In the process, they created a cascading series of new problems.

When they ordered businesses to close, government officials did not tell us the alternatives that they had considered and why those alternatives had been rejected. They did not mention the potential problems that a shutdown might cause. Instead, they presented only one policy: stay home, work safe, or else. Government officials acted to address the immediate problem—protecting "the public" from COVID.

As an example of an alternative to lockdowns, government officials could have shared information with citizens and made recommendations for mitigating the risk. Individuals and businesses would have been free to evaluate the risks based on their personal context and then act on their decisions. Businesses would have had a vested interest in finding innovative ways to protect employees and customers. But government officials said nothing about alternatives.

As the lockdowns poignantly illustrated, in focusing on "the public," (or any other collective) the Progressive framework inevitably harms the individuals who comprise the public.

The Progressive Framework Is Anti-Individual

The Progressive framework subordinates the individual—every individual—to the collective. That thinking method demands that the individual sacrifice his values and ambitions—his life— to the group. When the collective is the standard, what happens to the individual is regarded as irrelevant. When put into practice, this framework unleashes a power struggle as various groups compete to influence government officials and secure political favors.

The favors dispensed by government officials always come at the expense of others—non-members of the favored group. Tenants receive the favor of rent control at the expense of landlords who can only increase rents by an amount dictated by government. Low- and moderate-income households receive the favor of below-market rate housing imposed by inclusionary zoning at the expense of their neighbors who must pay higher rents to subsidize "affordable housing."

Often these favors are justified as "empowering" the beneficiaries or "balancing the power" between two groups. The truth is these favors give the group power over individuals. These favors grant the collective the authority to control the actions of other individuals.

This is precisely what the Progressive framework demands. Individuals, to repeat the words of James Edwin Creighton, have value "just in so far as they embody and express the life and purpose of a larger social whole of which they are members." The Progressive framework relegates the individual to second-class status. The collective reigns supreme.

When the alleged well-being of the group serves as the standard, the individual is necessarily harmed. He is forced to sacrifice for others, regardless of his own values and desires. His interests and aspirations are secondary to the collective's demands.

The Progressive framework has dominated housing and related policies for more than a century. That thinking method is the cause of the housing crisis. If we truly wish to solve the crisis, then we must reject that anti-individual framework. In its place we must adopt a pro-individual framework, a thinking method that empowers the individual with control over his own life, not the lives of others.

ESTABLISHING A PRO-INDIVIDUAL FRAMEWORK

Individuals occupy housing units. Groups do not. Individuals are the ones struggling to find safe, decent, and affordable housing. Groups are not. Individuals have jobs. Groups do not. If we want to help individuals flourish, then we must embrace a framework that is pro-individual in regard to every issue, including housing.

If we truly want to solve the affordable housing crisis, then we must begin by embracing a standard that applies to all individuals, not just the members of some favored group. We must be clear about what we want to achieve, and it must be a goal that is reasonable and achievable. If, like my tenant, we select an objective that is unreasonable, then we doom ourselves to failure. We are striving for something that is unattainable. As my tenant illustrated, choosing the wrong objective will skew our evaluation of the facts and the decisions that we will make. We will choose actions that do not serve our best interests. This is true of the individual's decisions, and it is true of decisions regarding government policy.

A pro-individual framework must consider the full context—all of the relevant facts. This is neither easy nor automatic. We must exert effort to identify how a policy will impact other issues, the long-term consequences, and the costs. If we drop context, we blind ourselves to the best solutions and ignore potential problems. We may adopt policies that do more harm than good.

Finally, a pro-individual framework will guide us to consider the pros and cons of various alternatives. We will not tenaciously cling to failed policies, nor will we dismiss alternatives without a full consideration of their benefits and costs. We cannot look only at the pros of popular policies and the negatives of unpopular policies.

This framework provides us with the method to solve the housing crisis. The first step is to establish a pro-individual standard.

A Pro-Individual Standard

If we want individuals, no matter their race, sex, religion, or income level, to be able pursue their own dreams and goals, then we cannot and should not call on them to sacrifice their aspirations and values for others. If they must sacrifice their dreams and ambitions, they cannot pursue their own happiness. If we want individuals to be able to thrive and live flourishing lives, the group is not the appropriate standard. If we want individuals—every individual—to be able to live the life he chooses, then we must reject the group—any group—as the standard.

If we want to enable individuals to live the most fulfilling life possible, then our standard must be applicable to all individuals—tenants and landlords, rich and poor, black and white, male and female, gays and heterosexuals. If our standard only applies to some, but not all individuals, then we will ultimately be setting one group or another as the standard. We must reject the collectivism of the Progressive framework. In its place, we must embrace individualism.

Individualism regards each individual as a sovereign being with an unalienable right to life, liberty, and the pursuit of his happiness. The individualist recognizes that each individual possesses the same rights. The Declaration of Independence stated the essence of individualism.

All individuals, the Declaration proclaims, are endowed with certain unalienable rights. Every individual—tenants and landlords, rich and poor, black and white, male or female, gays and heterosexuals—has a right to live as he chooses, to be free to act as he deems best, to pursue his own personal happiness. Individual rights are the proper standard for evaluating public policies, because only individual rights protect the freedom of each person to live as he desires, so long as he respects the freedom of others to do the same.

Rights pertain to freedom of action. Rights protect our freedom to act as we judge best in the pursuit of the values we need and desire. There is no such thing as a right to a value; there is only the right to take the actions necessary to produce or earn a value. We have a right to sew or purchase a shirt. We do not have a right to shirts. In regard to housing, each individual has a right to produce or earn the housing that he desires, but we do not have a right to housing. In regard to housing policy, our standard must be the protection of each individual's freedom to produce or earn the housing he wants. This standard applies to every individual, tenant and landlord, black and white, rich and poor, male and female, gay and heterosexual.

Individual rights empower the individual—every individual—with control over his own life. Individual rights protect the individual's freedom to act as he deems best in the pursuit of the values that he needs and desires without physical interference from others. Individual rights enable each individual to flourish if he has the ambition to do so and he exerts the necessary effort.

It is important to understand that individual rights are not a license to act on any whim or desire. The rights of others place boundaries on what we may morally do. The rights of others prohibit us from using physical force to prevent them from acting as they choose. If an individual is tied up, threatened with a gun, or has his property stolen, physical force (or the threat thereof) has prevented him from acting on his own judgment.

When the group is the standard, physical force is used to compel individuals to act as the group demands and dictates. When the group is the standard, physical force is used to control the actions of individuals. When individual rights is the standard, then each individual has the freedom to control his own life, and others are prohibited from using physical force to control or interfere with his actions.

As an example, individual rights protect the freedom of landlords to establish whatever terms and conditions they think appropriate for their rental properties. At the same time, individual rights protect the freedom of tenants to agree with those terms and conditions, negotiate terms and conditions more to their liking, or move. Individual rights protect the freedom of both the landlord and the tenant to act on their own judgment. Rights protect our freedom to associate with others voluntarily and to the benefit of all involved.

That tenants may not like their alternatives does not mean that their rights have been violated. Rights pertain to freedom of action, not the guaranteed satisfaction of our every desire. Raising the rent is not an act of physical force. Refusing to renew a lease is not a violation of a tenant's rights. Prohibiting pets is not an act of physical force.

In contrast, the myriad laws being enacted to protect "tenants' rights" are an act of physical force. Such laws compel landlords to act as government officials dictate, and violators are subject to fines, jail, or both. "Tenants' rights" laws force landlords to act contrary to their own judgment.

As another example, individual rights protect the freedom of individuals to offer the services of their choosing. At the same time, individual rights protect the freedom of consumers to hire the service provider or not. Individual rights protect the freedom of both the producer and the consumer to act on their own judgment. Rights protect our freedom to associate with others voluntarily and to the benefit of all involved.

In contrast, occupational licensing laws prohibit individuals from entering many professions without first obtaining the government's permission. Consumers are prohibited from hiring unlicensed individuals. Occupational licensing prohibits service providers and consumers from acting as they deem best. Violators are subject to fines, jail, or both.

Identifying the correct standard is only the starting point in establishing the proper framework. If we want to make the best choices, then we must consider all of the relevant facts. We must consider the big picture—the full context.

A Pro-Individual Framework Considers The Full Context

The full context means all of the relevant facts. If we ignore or evade relevant facts, then we are engaging in willful and intentional self-blindness. We will not reach the best conclusions. Considering the full context means that we cannot look at a problem or issue in isolation. We must identify how a particular policy will impact other issues. We must also identify the long-term consequences of a policy, not just the immediate results.

To consider the full context requires an active mind—a mind willing and able to consider new or challenging ideas critically and objectively. In contrast, a passive mind clings to whatever ideas it holds and stubbornly refuses to consider new information. An active mind seeks the truth and welcomes new facts and ideas. A passive mind rejects anything that challenges its previous conclusions. An active mind seeks to integrate issues. A passive mind regards each issue as isolated. An active mind can solve the housing crisis. A passive mind will simply repeat the slogans of the past and support the policies that have failed for decades.

The affordability of housing isn't an isolated issue. While

there are many factors that contribute to the cost of housing, factors other than the cost of building new housing determines which housing is affordable to a particular individual. If we truly want to solve the housing crisis, then we must consider all of the factors relevant to the affordability of housing. And one of the most significant of those factors is income.

It should be obvious that a person with an income of $25,000 is going to struggle to attain adequate housing, along with food, health care, clothing, transportation, and other basic necessities. Such individuals are not going to have the same housing options as a person making $100,000. If we really want to help low-income individuals obtain affordable housing, then we must seek to understand all of the factors involved, including why their income is so low. The affordability of housing is a function of both income and the price of housing.

Housing advocates frequently state that housing prices keep rising while wages have stagnated. And while they cite numerous studies and reports to support their claim, we must dig deeper if we want to consider the full context.

First, we must be clear about what these statistics really mean. For example, most studies on wages look at particular groups of employees, such as factory workers or secretarial support. They then compare wages for these groups between two particular points in time and adjust for inflation. Many of these studies find that wages have increased very little over time.

The problem with this approach is that it is focused on groups, not individuals. A particular job in a factory may pay about the same as it did twenty years ago, but the same individuals who performed those jobs twenty years ago are probably not performing them today. Individuals often get promoted or move to another company with a higher paying job. To focus on the group is to ignore the full context—what is happening with individuals.

In their book, *Equal is Unfair*, Don Watkins and Yaron Brook address the claim of stagnating wages and provide a proper way to compare wages over time:

> The claim that the middle class has stagnated since 1979 does not mean that someone who started working in 1979 is making the same amount of money today. That is seldom true. There are basically two ways to measure what happens to individuals over time. One way involves using what's called cohort data. Using this method, we can look at what people between the ages of, say, 20 to 30 earned in 1979 and compare that to what 48- to 59-year-olds earned in 2007.[16]

Watkins and Brook go on to note that economist Stephen J. Rose examined incomes for married couples in 1979 and 2007. He found that the median income for such couples rose from $55,600 in 1979 to $81,000 in 2007, an increase of nearly 46 percent. When Rose looked at what happened to specific individuals, he found that those who were twenty to thirty-one years old in 1979 were earning 44 percent more in 2007. These findings demonstrate that when we only look at groups, rather than the individuals comprising those groups, we can reach a very misleading and inaccurate conclusion.

Second, we must look at what actions individuals are taking to improve their earning potential. If a worker makes little or no effort to improve his job skills or learn new skills, his earning potential is going to be lower than an individual who takes such actions. Every individual has an ongoing choice to stagnate or to grow, and we cannot ignore the role that those choices have on an individual's income, and thus, housing affordability. To ignore the role that myriad choices play in the affordability of housing is to drop context. Yet, this is an issue that housing advocates seldom discuss. It is the elephant in the room, and if we want to successfully solve the affordable housing crisis, it must be addressed.

If we fail to consider all of the relevant facts—if we drop context—then important information does not enter into our evaluation. We will attempt to make a good decision while ignoring facts that could enlighten us. When we drop context, bad decisions are almost guaranteed to follow. When we drop context and look at issues in isolation, it is likely that we will make policy decisions in one area that have a detrimental impact in another. When we drop context, we look only at the easily seen and identified. Considering the full context means connecting and integrating all of the facts and issues pertaining to the topic we are considering.

It isn't easy to identify and consider the full context. It takes effort, and that effort isn't automatic. One must consciously choose to identify all of the related issues and all of the relevant information, and then one must engage in the effort to discover that information and integrate it. In doing so, one can't start with a preconceived conclusion that one wants to find evidence to support. One must look at the evidence and then draw conclusions based on the evidence. In a court of law, justice demands that one consider all of the evidence and nothing but the evidence. In considering housing policy (or any policy or idea), justice demands that we do the same.

In regard to the affordability of housing, there are many factors that play a role. As mentioned, an individual's income is one factor. Other factors include the cost of land, the labor and material costs to build new housing, and for rental housing, the cost of operation. Many public policies have both direct and indirect effects on each of these factors, as well as others. The relationship between all of these policies must be considered. And then we must consider the pros and cons of alternative policies.

A Pro-Individual Framework Considers The Pros And Cons Of Alternatives

Often, we are presented with false alternatives. We are told that we must choose between A and B, and the fact that a C and D exist is not mentioned or considered. The tactic of false alternatives is frequently used in debates over a policy proposal. By limiting the alternatives that are presented, supporters of a proposal seek to prevent policies that they oppose from even being considered.

Consider claim made by defenders of single-family zoning when Joe Biden suggested that he might require municipalities that receive federal funds to relax zoning regulations. Former New York Lt. Gov. Betsy McCaughey wrote, "What he really wants is to put the federal government in charge of local zoning and to install apartment buildings throughout single-family-home neighborhoods."[17] Biden's proposal, she went on to write, "creates a gigantic pot of taxpayer funds to hand out to towns that surrender self-rule. That's a mistake. Local control is vital. Towns can take into account the availability of public transportation, school capacity and proximity to employment. Uncle Sam has no clue."

McCaughey, like most defenders of single-family zoning, presents the false alternatives of federal land-use regulations or local government land-use regulations. A third alternative —no government land-use regulations—isn't even mentioned. She offers us the choice between federal control of our property and local control of our property and ignores the alternative of returning control to the property owner. This isn't surprising, because like all defenders of single-family zoning, McCaughey's standard is the group—the community.

Presented with these alternatives, most people would prefer local control. It is much easier to express one's views and influence policy makers at the local level. But many property owners would prefer that no government agency dictate what they can and cannot do with their land. They would prefer a reduction in government controls over their property. This is an alternative that is seldom considered.

A pro-individual framework helps us identify false alternatives. In the above example, both of the alternatives presented involve the threat of physical force to control how individuals use their land. Land-use regulations, whether federal or local, dictate how a parcel of land may be used. Violators are subject to fines (having one's money seized), jail (the equivalent of being tied up), or both. The threat of force prevents the individual from acting on his own judgment, just as a robber or kidnapper does.

An individualistic framework rejects any policy that seeks to control others through physical force. An individualistic framework recognizes the fact that alternatives to rights-violating policies always exist. However, recognizing that alternatives must exist is one thing. Identifying what those alternatives are is something else entirely. It isn't always easy to identify rights-respecting alternatives. In some instances, the rights-respecting alternative is simply refraining from policies that control individuals and violate their rights.

There will be those who will cling to the Progressive framework and find this unacceptable. They will demand that mandates and prohibitions be used to control individuals. And as long as they embrace an anti-individual framework, they will continue to do so.

In addressing the housing crisis, we face the alternatives of an anti-individual framework and a pro-individual framework. These are not false alternatives. One either regards the individual as subordinate to the group, or one holds that individuals have unalienable rights. There is no middle ground. There are no other alternatives. Either all individuals possess rights, or none do.

Because housing isn't an isolated issue, we must also consider alternatives regarding other issues that impact the affordability of housing. We must identify policies that restrict or impede an individual's ability to improve his income, and thus, the affordability of housing. For example, laws regarding occupational licensing, minimum wage, and labor unions frequently prevent individuals from entering a profession or obtaining job skills (we will examine these issues in later chapters.). These laws are particularly destructive to the ambitious poor because they arbitrarily eliminate opportunities to improve one's earning potential. We must apply a pro-individual framework to each of these policy issues as well.

If we follow the proper framework, we can solve the affordable housing crisis. And we can solve it in a manner that is moral and just for everyone.

PART 2

The Past

*If your only tool is a hammer then every problem
looks like a nail.* Abraham Maslow

During the second half of the nineteenth century, America was transformed from an agrarian economy to an industrial economy. This transformation brought with it changes in nearly every aspect of life. Many found these changes undesirable and they sought to reform America. The reform movement was first led by the Populists, and then the Progressives led the effort.

The Progressive framework was applied to myriad problems, both real and imagined. As the influence of collectivism spread, the scope and powers of government expanded significantly during the first half of the twentieth century. A partial list of the new agencies and departments established by the federal government during this period would include the Food and Drug Administration (1906), the Federal Reserve (1913), the Federal Trade Commission (1914, the Federal Housing Administration (1934), the Securities and Exchange Commission (1934), and the National Labor Relations Board (1935). During this period, an Amendment to the Constitution was ratified and created the nation's first income tax (1913) and in 1920 Prohibition took effect.

On the state and local level, zoning laws were passed in hundreds of cities across the nation prior to World War II, most states began regulating banks, the government school system adopted Progressive education, and regulations were imposed on myriad businesses.

Government's only tool is force. The reformers were disenchanted with the choices that many individuals were making. They wanted government to compel actions that they—the reformers—thought more appropriate.

Many of these new agencies and laws had an impact on housing, both directly and indirectly. All were the result of the Progressive framework.

SINGLE-FAMILY ZONING

Over the past few decades, a growing number of economists and scholars have examined how government policies, and particularly single-family zoning, have contributed to the affordable housing shortage. While there is not universal agreement on how these policies have impacted affordable housing, there is a general agreement that single-family zoning has been a significant factor in the housing crisis.

Most land-use regulations, such as single-family zoning, were enacted by local governments during the Progressive Era. While there can be significant differences between locales, all zoning laws are a result of the Progressive framework. All place restrictions and controls on the use of land for the purpose of promoting and protecting "community values." All subordinate the individual to the collective.

The Birth Of Zoning

At the beginning of the twentieth century, most Americans were renters. Buying a house was a difficult process. Few banks offered home mortgages. Those that did often required a down payment of 50 percent and amortized the loan over a short period—five to seven years was typical. Compared to today's thirty-year mortgages that require 20 percent or less as a down payment, it is easy to understand why most Americans rented.

At the time, transportation was also much different than it is today. The automobile was unaffordable for most

Americans, and they relied on trolleys, horses, bicycles, and walking for transportation. Because of the limitations of transportation at the time, most neighborhoods were a mixture of commercial enterprises and housing. Bakeries, butchers, produce stands, and other essential businesses operated in close proximity to houses and apartments.

The housing options available were also quite different from today. Small apartment buildings, townhomes, duplexes, rooming houses, cottages, and more usually existed in a neighborhood, and often on the same block. However, as cities rapidly grew in the late nineteenth and early twentieth centuries, many began to consider these mixed land uses "incompatible" and undesirable. Cities began enacting land-use regulations in response.

The first of these regulations were enacted in California. In 1880, San Francisco enacted an ordinance prohibiting laundries from operating in a wooden building without a permit from city officials. Ostensibly, the ordinance was a safety measure. In fact, it was a thinly veiled attempt to segregate certain individuals. When the law was enacted, about two-thirds of the city's three-hundred-twenty laundries were owned by individuals of Chinese descent. When the Chinese owners applied for a permit, only one of those applications was approved. Of the non-Chinese applicants, all but one received a city permit. The United States Supreme Court struck down the law in 1886, but other cities were soon enacting land-use regulations.

In 1908, Los Angeles passed the nation's first zoning ordinance. Unlike later zoning laws, the zoning map did not apply to every parcel of land in the entire city. The law did establish residential and industrial districts, and prohibited laundries, lumber yards, and any business using motors from being located in residential areas, a provision that forced many businesses to relocate. Other cities soon followed with their own zoning ordinances modeled on the Los Angeles law, and by 1913 more than twenty other cities were regulating land uses.

When the 1880 ordinance enacted in San Francisco was struck down, the Court noted that the ordinance was not explicitly racist. However, the Court found that the intention of the law and its implementation were clearly designed to prevent Chinese laundries from operating in the city. While the Supreme Court did not reject land-use regulations per se, they did reject land-use regulations founded on racism. Despite this ruling, between 1910 and 1917, cities across the nation enacted zoning ordinances that were explicitly racist.

The first city to enact such an ordinance was Baltimore in 1910. That ordinance prohibited blacks from living in neighborhoods that were predominantly white and vice versa. Over the next few years, nearly a dozen cities—including Louisville—enacted racial zoning laws to segregate whites and minorities.

Similar to the Baltimore ordinance, the law in Louisville prohibited blacks from owning or occupying real property in areas that were majority white and vice versa. The Jim Crow-style ordinance was opposed by many white businessmen. They found it morally repugnant and bad for business. One of those businessmen was Charles Buchanan, a realtor and real estate developer.

William Warley, a black attorney, teamed up with Charles Buchanan to challenge the Louisville zoning ordinance in court. Buchanan purchased a vacant parcel of land in a white neighborhood. Warley agreed to buy the land from Buchanan and attached a condition to his offer:

> It is understood that I am purchasing the above property for the purpose of having erected thereon a house which I propose to make my residence, and it is a distinct part of this agreement that I shall not be required to accept a deed to the above property or to pay for said property unless I have the right under the laws of the State of Kentucky and the City of Louisville to occupy said property as a residence.[18]

Buchanan accepted the offer, but Warley was unable to complete the transaction because of the zoning ordinance. As the two men had planned, Buchanan sued Warley for breach of contract. The case eventually reached the United States Supreme Court.

In *Buchanan v. Warley*, the Court unanimously declared that race-based zoning was unconstitutional. "Colored persons," the decision stated, "are citizens of the United States and have the right to purchase property and enjoy and use the same without laws discriminating against them solely on the account of race." Warley lost the case, but he accomplished what he had intended.

The ruling in *Buchanan* did not stop Indianapolis, Birmingham, New Orleans, and other cities from passing explicitly race-based zoning ordinances. Some cities, such as Atlanta, Austin, and Norfolk, did not pass ordinances explicitly based on race, but they did consider race in making zoning decisions, a practice that continued for decades after *Buchanan*.

As another example of race-based zoning, in 1924 Richmond, Virginia passed an ordinance that prohibited individuals from living on a street where they were ineligible to marry a majority of those already living there. At the time, interracial marriage was illegal in Virginia. The ordinance banned blacks from white neighborhoods in an underhanded attempt to sidestep *Buchanan*.

These race-based ordinances were founded on the Progressive framework and were grossly unjust. Rather than treat individuals equally before the law, such laws prevented individuals from taking certain actions, not because they had done something wrong, but solely because of skin color. Both black and white individuals were subordinate to the group. While the explicitly racist provisions of zoning disappeared long ago, zoning continues to be defended by those embracing the Progressive framework.

Today, many Progressives and many conservatives defend zoning as a way to promote and protect "community values." The defenders want to keep multi-family housing— i.e., less expensive housing—out of their neighborhood. This perpetuates economic segregation by making it unaffordable for low- and moderate-income individuals to find housing in more desirable neighborhoods.

Zoning was originally used to keep non-whites out of white neighborhoods. Today it is used to keep low- and moderate-income individuals out of middle- and upper-income neighborhoods. Regardless of the particular group that is being "protected" by zoning, individuals are subordinated to the collective.

Zoning Goes Mainstream

While some cities continued to pass race-based zoning, others found less explicit means for using zoning to keep blacks and other minorities out of white neighborhoods. As one example, in 1916, Berkeley, California passed what is believed to be the first single-family zoning ordinance in the nation. The law dictated that only single-family homes could be built in much of the city. Because most blacks and other minorities could not afford to purchase a single-family home, the law essentially prohibited them from living in white neighborhoods.

In early 2021, the Berkley City Council unanimously voted to end single-family zoning in the city. At the time, one council member noted "that from the outset, zoning's sole purpose was to segregate by race, to the detriment of people of color."[19] From the beginning of zoning, the alleged well-being of the group—whites—was often the standard used to defend legally mandated racial segregation. Even when zoning wasn't explicitly racist, it was used to protect and promote "community values," which was simply a cover for racial and economic segregation.

In 1922, the Village of Euclid (a suburb of Cleveland), passed a zoning ordinance with the intention of keeping industry out of the village. Ambler Realty owned 68 acres in the village that it had planned to develop for industrial uses. That plan was negated by the zoning ordinance, and Ambler Realty sued.

In *Village of Euclid, Ohio v. Ambler Realty Co.*, 272 U.S. 365 (1926), the United States Supreme Court declared zoning a legitimate use of a city's police power to keep certain types of buildings out of residential areas. In the ruling, Justice George Sutherland referred to an apartment complex as "a mere parasite" on a neighborhood. This set the stage for single-family zoning to spread across the nation as a means to achieve both racial and economic segregation.

The "success" of single-family zoning in Berkeley, along with the ruling in *Euclid*, motivated other cities to adopt similar restrictions. Indeed, the *New York Times* once said that single-family zoning is "practically gospel in America."[20] Today, an estimated 75 percent or more of the land in nearly every city in the country is zoned for single-family homes.

While zoning ordinances were enacted by local governments, the federal government played a significant role in the increased use of zoning during the 1920s. In 1921, Secretary of Commerce Herbert Hoover organized an Advisory Committee on Zoning. The committee developed a manual explaining why every city should adopt a zoning ordinance, along with a model ordinance. Thousands of copies of the manual were distributed across the nation.

Two years after publishing its manual, the advisory committee adopted a code of ethics that included a warning: "a realtor should never be instrumental in introducing into a neighborhood . . . members of any race or nationality... whose presence will clearly be detrimental to property values in that neighborhood."[21] This "code of ethics" was simply an underhanded way to promote an unethical goal—housing segregation based on race. And the federal government wasn't alone in pressuring realtors to keep blacks out of white neighborhoods.

In 1919, states began licensing realtors. The stated purpose of the licensing was to protect home buyers— there were many unscrupulous individuals selling real estate to unwary buyers. Licensing, the public was told, would ensure that those selling real estate would be competent and trustworthy. Those wanting to become a realtor had to meet whatever criteria the licensing board established. In short, to become a realtor, one had to obtain the government's permission. Again, the individual was subordinated to the collective.

The licensing boards did more than establish the standards that had to be met to enter the profession. Like Hoover's advisory committee, many licensing boards explicitly prohibited realtors from selling a property in white neighborhoods to blacks. Those who did were subject to losing their real estate license and their livelihood.

On the one hand, local governments were prohibiting blacks from living in predominantly white neighborhoods. On the other hand, through licensing state governments were prohibiting realtors from selling property to blacks in areas that were majority white. In both instances, it was government that legally mandated racism and segregation. In both instances, violators were subject to severe penalties. In both instances, the alleged well-being of the group—whites— served as the rationalization for an injustice. The policies of both local governments and state licensing boards subordinated individuals—both whites and blacks—to the group. Most of these anti-individual policies remain in place today.

Each of the examples cited above is founded on the same premise: the interests of some group—the community, the neighborhood, whites—supersede the interests of individuals. Whenever the group serves as the standard of value, individuals are subordinated to that collective. Blacks who wanted to live in predominantly white neighborhoods were forced to sacrifice their interests to the group. Whites—whether realtors or property owners—who wanted to sell properties to blacks in white neighborhoods were forced to sacrifice their interests to the collective.

Fundamentally, the purpose of zoning (and every policy

using the group as the standard of value) is to compel the individual to act contrary to his own judgment. Under zoning, he can only use his property as the group permits. Every zoning ordinance is founded on the premise that the group is the standard. The Progressive framework shaped discussions regarding zoning from the beginning, and it continues to shape those discussions today.

For example, one website states, "Zoning allows the government to control the development of the land and ensure the public is satisfied with their community."[22] In other words, the alleged welfare of the group supersedes the welfare of individuals. Another website states, "Zoning is intended to regulate the use of private land for the common good. It establishes that the interests of private property owners must be balanced against the interests of the public."[23] In other words, the alleged interests of the collective—"the public"—supersede the interests of the individuals who comprise the public. The individual is subordinate to the group.

As a means of determining the "public interest," zoning boards usually conduct public hearings when zoning changes are proposed for a parcel of land. These hearings become a magnet for special interest groups, activists, and others to object to a project or make demands of the developer. As one example, community activists in New York City objected to a 55-story residential building, claiming that the developer had abused the zoning process. The building was nearing completion when a state judge ruled that the building was illegal and ordered the developer to remove the top floors. The developer had previously obtained all of the necessary permits from the city's zoning department, but the judge overruled that approval. So, even though the developer had met the city's demands, he was later ordered to meet the demands of the group—the community. The individual was subordinated to the collective. Fortunately, the judge's ruling was subsequently overturned, but this story is an example of how zoning forces individuals to sacrifice for the group.

In this example, and countless others, individuals are forced to comply with the demands and interests of the collective. Their own judgment and values are subordinate to the judgment and values of others, whether government officials or community activists. This is the inevitable result when the group serves as the standard of what is good. And the victims are not just developers and builders. Every consumer of housing, which means all of us, pays higher prices because of zoning. Virtually every activity within a municipality that involves the use of land—which is almost everything—is more expensive because of the controls and restrictions imposed by land-use regulations.

The Cost Of Zoning

A report issued by the Brookings Institution illustrates the costs imposed on builders, developers, and property owners by zoning. The report focused on land costs near rail stations in the Boston area.[24] Most of that land is zoned for single-family homes, and the cost of a lot is as high as $850,000 in one neighborhood. The entire cost of the land is reflected in the price for one housing unit.

However, if three townhomes were built on the same parcel of land, the land price per housing unit would be less than $300,000. The report correctly notes that even with this type of savings, homes would still remain unaffordable to low-income families. But it illustrates the significant role that single-family zoning has on housing costs. And this is hardly the only impact zoning and land-use regulations have on housing affordability.

Richard N. Maier, an executive at home builder DR Horton, detailed the cost of regulations on one property in Austin, Texas.[25] In his article, Maier lists the costs of five city regulations:

1. Historic Preservation-- $16,226
2. Heritage Tree Ordinance-- $2,742

3. Impervious Cover-- $79,800
4. Storm Water Pollution Protection-- $1,563
5. The "McMansion" Ordinance-- $12,500

The cost of these regulations came to $112,831! Maier noted that the average builder operates on a margin of 18 percent, which could bring the total cost of regulations to $137,598. This is the amount that the home price will be increased simply to pay for government regulations. At the time Maier wrote, Zillow reported that the median home price in Austin was $326,000.[26] The cost of regulations on this one property represents more than 40 percent of the median home price.

If the cost of regulations alone in Austin is $137,598, a builder cannot construct new homes for low-income families. Simply meeting government dictates raises the cost of construction beyond the means of low-income families. Only a fool would try to build such housing, and he wouldn't build many homes because he'd run out of money very quickly. Building new housing for low-income families under such conditions is far beyond risky—it is financial suicide. And Austin is not unique.

In 2008, University of Washington professor Theo Eicher found that land-use regulations imposed by the city of Seattle and the state of Washington increased the cost of a home by $200,000! At that time, the median home price in Seattle was $450,000, which means that land-use regulations increased the cost of a home by 44 percent. As an example of one regulation, in 2005 Seattle imposed a $15-per-square-foot surcharge on developers in order to subsidize low-income housing. That regulation alone added $9,000 to the cost of a 600-square-foot downtown condominium.[27]

As I noted earlier, economists, scholars, and public officials are increasingly understanding the economic impracticality of some land-use regulations. However, because they focus on the economic consequences, many believe that land-use regulations are a necessary evil. And so, they seek to find a balance between protecting "community values" and the impact those regulations have on housing prices. They seek to eliminate or reduce one destructive form of zoning while retaining other destructive land-use regulations.

The truth is, no matter what balance is struck, so long as the group remains the standard, zoning will be considered necessary. There is no balance between an anti-individual framework and a pro-individual framework, between collectivism and individualism. So long as the group is the standard, land-use regulations will continue to be supported as a tool to compel individuals to sacrifice for the collective. The solution is to reject the idea that the group—any group—should serve as the standard.

Relaxing or repealing single-family zoning regulations is a start. But if we truly want affordable housing for all, then we must eliminate all of the regulations that impose arbitrary costs on builders and developers.

The Freedom To Produce And Trade

Fundamentally, the shortage of housing for low- and moderate-income households is an issue of supply. The demand for affordable housing greatly exceeds the supply. The supply can only be increased through additional production, i.e., by building more housing.

As we have seen, zoning adds substantial costs to the construction of new housing. Along with the costs imposed by other regulations, it is impossible for builders and developers to produce housing that is affordable for low- and moderate-income households.

In all of its forms, zoning prohibits the freedom to produce and trade. In the early years of zoning, property owners in predominantly white neighborhoods could not sell to blacks, and vice versa. Realtors were prohibited from arranging such trades. Individuals were not free to trade to the mutual benefit of all parties. Individuals could only produce and trade as the group allowed.

Today, zoning continues to restrict the freedom to produce and trade. Single-family zoning makes it illegal to build any kind of housing other than single-family homes. Because of zoning, builders and developers are not free to produce housing where individuals want to live. Instead, they can only produce housing of the type allowed by government.

A supply shortage cannot be remedied by shackling producers and imposing enormous costs on them. If we wish to increase the supply of affordable housing, then we must restore the freedom to produce and trade. To free housing producers, we must abolish all forms of land-use regulation, including single-family zoning.

Freeing housing producers does not mean that neighborhoods will be overrun by sprawling apartment complexes and oil refineries. (In Chapter 14 we will look at non-coercive methods for addressing these issues.) It does mean that builders and developers can build the types of housing that individuals want in the places that they want to live. It means that builders and developers, and hence consumers, won't be forced to pay the outrageous costs of regulations.

When zoning was first proposed, the Progressive framework dominated the discussion. That framework continues to dominate discussions of zoning and housing policy to this day. The defense of zoning begins with the wrong standard—the group. Whether it is whites, the community, or some other group, the alleged well-being of the collective is the standard by which zoning is evaluated. As a result, zoning is examined as an isolated policy with no impact on other issues. The benefits to the group are touted while the harm to non-members is dismissed or evaded. Finally, zoning is so deeply entrenched in America that alternatives are not even considered. And, in the case of single-family zoning, alternatives such as duplexes or "granny flats" are illegal.

If we truly want to solve the housing crisis, then we must adopt a new framework. We must think about single-family zoning and other land-use regulations in a fresh way. We must reject the collectivist framework and embrace the individualist framework.

The manufacturers of virtually every consumer product offer a range of products from the low-end to the high-end. There is no rational reason to believe that housing producers won't do the same. But first, they must be free to do so.

FEDERAL HOUSING SUBSIDIES

For nearly one hundred years, the federal government has had two distinct, though often overlapping, priorities regarding housing. The first set of priorities focuses primarily on rental housing for low- and moderate-income families. The resulting programs have sought to increase the supply of low-income rental housing through subsidies, grants, and tax credits. The second set of priorities has focused on helping families purchase a home. Initially, this effort focused on middle-class white families. In recent years, the focus has shifted to low- and moderate-income families, with a particular emphasis on blacks and Latinos.

Numerous government agencies are involved in shaping and implementing housing policy. The most prominent are the Department of Housing and Urban Development (HUD), the Federal Housing Administration (FHA), the government sponsored enterprises known as Fannie Mae and Freddie Mac, and the Federal Housing Finance Agency, which oversees and regulates Fannie Mae and Freddie Mac. Another institution—the Federal Reserve—also exerts considerable influence over the implementation of housing policies by controlling available credit. We will examine the Federal Reserve in the next chapter.

To fully address these agencies and the history of federal housing subsidies is far beyond the scope of this book. My purpose here isn't a comprehensive history, but to demonstrate how the Progressive framework has driven past policy decisions and contributed to the current housing crisis.

Subsidizing Rental Housing

The federal government's first significant efforts to help low-income renters came during the Great Depression with the passage of the National Industrial Recovery Act in 1933. Among other provisions, the act directed the Public Works Administration (PWA) to develop a program for the "construction, reconstruction, alteration, or repair under public regulation or control of low-cost housing and slum clearance projects …" The program quickly floundered and Harold Ickes, the PWA Administrator, ordered the agency to directly build low-income housing. This set the stage for the Housing Act of 1937, which provided subsidies to local public housing agencies to improve the living conditions of low-income families.

Twelve years later, the government expanded its role in low-income housing with the Housing Act of 1949. This sweeping legislation included financing for slum clearance programs (often called urban renewal) in American cities and funding for more than 800,000 public housing units by 1955. In cities across the nation thousands of homes were demolished to make way for new public housing buildings and other projects. Even though the government frequently built new housing for the displaced residents, most of the projects resulted in a net loss of housing. As one example, development of the Lincoln Center in New York City required the demolition of 7,000 apartments. Only 4,400 were built to replace them.

Like most of the federal government's housing policies, the grand goals of the Housing Act of 1949 were never realized. By 1955 many cities were experiencing a severe shortage of low-income housing, despite the efforts of the federal government. This shouldn't have been a surprise since thousands of affordable homes were demolished and not replaced. "Urban renewal" destroyed more housing than it created. And, as the public housing projects fell into disrepair and developed into a breeding ground for crime, it became clear that this policy was an abject failure.

The government's efforts regarding low-income housing were guided by the same Progressive framework that gave rise to zoning. Zoning advocates saw "incompatible" land uses and integrated neighborhoods as a problem. Their solution was to outlaw land uses that they deemed undesirable. The advocates of urban renewal saw tenements and slums as unfit for human habitation. Their solution was to demolish the substandard housing and replace it with something they deemed more suitable. Both sets of advocates focused on the alleged benefits to a particular group, while ignoring the actual consequences to individuals. Both zoning and urban renewal subordinated individuals to the collective, and countless individuals suffered.

The advocates of zoning and urban renewal asserted a standard of what is good and what is bad, and then they imposed that standard on everyone else. To the crusaders, incompatible land uses and substandard housing had to be eliminated. The advocates presumed to know what was best for individuals, and then they used the coercive power of government to impose their values upon others. The result was not urban renewal. Instead, tens of thousands of affordable housing units were demolished, and tens of thousands of individuals were displaced.

The failures of public housing projects led to the Housing Act of 1954, which offered subsidies to developers to build low-income housing by providing mortgages insured by the Federal Housing Administration. This marked a substantial change in the government's approach to low-income housing. Rather than build such housing itself, government would offer financial incentives to private developers. However, the bill was expanded to include commercial and industrial development as well as residential development. This accelerated urban renewal projects to rejuvenate inner-city neighborhoods beginning in the late 1950s.

One reason why many inner-city neighborhoods fell into disrepair was the growing popularity of suburbs (this topic will be more fully addressed in Chapter 7). As middle-class, white families moved out of the city, the tax base decreased. Government began neglecting the infrastructure in poorer and predominantly minority neighborhoods. With private investment capital moving to the suburbs, inner-city neighborhoods began to deteriorate.

In many cities, government officials and business leaders worked together in seeking federal funding for new development. The local governments benefited from redevelopment through increased tax revenues. The private businesses benefited because it was easier and less expensive to acquire land for new development. Municipal governments often aided developers by seizing private property through eminent domain and then selling it to developers.

In many instances, the housing needs of the displaced weren't addressed, and once again, affordable housing for low-income households was reduced. As an example, 1,500 homes, 144 businesses, and 16 churches were bulldozed in the Poletown neighborhood of Detroit for a General Motors plant. The destruction of private homes and businesses was considered a justified use of eminent domain because it served the interests of the group—"the public." The individuals who owned those homes and businesses were forced to sacrifice their well-being to that of "the public."

With the Housing Act of 1954, the federal government began to rely on private businesses to produce low-income housing. In 1974, that effort was expanded when housing vouchers were approved by Congress. The Housing Choice Voucher Program provides direct housing assistance to renters that they can use to rent private housing. Participants in the program pay 30 percent to 40 percent of their income for housing, and the government pays the remainder of the rent. The program enables participants to rent the type of housing they desire, such as an apartment, a townhouse, a condominium, or a single-family home. The program allows low-income families to obtain subsidized housing outside of public housing projects. Today, more than two million households receive housing voucher subsidies.

A second program, the Low-Income Housing Tax Credit (LIHTC), was enacted as a part of the Tax Reform Act of 1986. The LIHTC program awards grants to cities and states to issue tax credits for the acquisition, rehabilitation, or new construction of rental housing targeted for lower-income households. From the program's inception through 2018, more than three million units were built under the program.

The LIHTC program implicitly acknowledges that building low-income housing is not generally profitable. If it were, developers would build such housing. Tax credits, like subsidies, are essentially a bribe to incentivize actions that an individual would not otherwise undertake. Tax credits and subsidies can turn an unprofitable project into a profitable endeavor. The government wants developers to build more housing for low-income families, but it would be impractical, if not impossible, to force developers to do so. And so, the government resorts to—i.e., bribery—to motivate developers to act as the government prefers.

Unfortunately, few policy makers bother to understand why it is unprofitable to build low-income housing. Instead of removing the obstacles, such as single-family zoning, they provide tax credits and subsidies. If the obstacles to producing housing were removed, subsidies to build more housing would not be needed. Because of the Progressive framework that they embrace they look at the problem in isolation, and subsidies seem to be the only tenable solution to achieve the results that they desire. Alternatives are not even considered. And the same is true of home ownership.

Subsidies For Home Ownership

Government's foray into housing during the Great Depression was not limited to helping low-income families obtain housing. In 1933, the Home Owners' Loan Corporation (HOLC) was formed to buy troubled mortgages (the borrower was behind on his payments) and then refinanced those loans for fifteen years (and later twenty-five years). Up to this time, most home loans were for five to seven years. By extending the time to repay the loans, HOLC significantly lowered the homeowner's monthly payment and allowed many to retain their home.

HOLC soon developed color-coded maps of every metropolitan area in the country to help assess which loans to purchase. Green areas were deemed safe, and red areas were deemed the riskiest, a policy that gave rise to the term "redlining." It was not a coincidence that nearly every neighborhood that wasn't predominantly white was assigned a red designation.

HOLC was not making lending decisions on the basis of credit worthiness because that would require evaluating each individual applicant. Instead, HOLC made decisions almost entirely on the basis of skin color—that is, membership in the favored group. It was an explicit policy of HOLC for government to provide subsidies for one group—whites—while denying those benefits to non-white individuals. And it wouldn't be the last federal agency to do so.

The Depression had destroyed the banking industry, and there were virtually no new home mortgages available. The Federal Housing Administration (FHA) was created in 1934 to insure mortgages. If a loan insured by FHA goes into default, FHA will pay the lender the outstanding balance. This eliminates a great deal of risk from lenders and helps stimulate lending. FHA mortgage insurance is a subsidy for home buyers, who would otherwise have to obtain private mortgage insurance, pay higher fees and interest rates, or make a larger downpayment.

FHA adopted HOLC's system of color-coded maps to determine which mortgages to insure, but FHA went a step further. The agency's underwriting manual prohibited loans to blacks, as well as loans to whites wanting to buy a home in a neighborhood that wasn't exclusively white. The explicit purpose was to create and maintain racial segregation by subsidizing home ownership for whites while denying the same opportunities to other individuals.

These policies were justified on the false belief that the presence of blacks in a neighborhood depressed property values. While this view was widely held, actual facts demonstrated that it simply wasn't true. As Richard Rothstein writes in *The Color of Law*,

> In 1948 an FHA official published a report asserting that "the infiltration of Negro owner-occupants has tended to appreciate property values and neighborhood stability." A 1952 study of sales in San Francisco compared prices in racially changing neighborhoods with those in a control group of racially stable neighborhoods. Published in the Appraisal Journal, a periodical with which housing practitioners, including FHA officials, would have been familiar, it concluded that "[t]hese results do not show that any deterioration in market prices occurred following changes in the racial pattern." Indeed, the study confirmed that because African Americans were willing to pay more than whites for similar housing, property values in neighborhoods where African Americans could purchase increased more often than they declined." This shouldn't be surprising. Demand for housing in integrated neighborhoods rose, and with it, values.[28]

True to the Progressive framework, policy decisions were made without considering all of the facts—the full context. Instead, government officials looked only at those facts that supported their unjust policies and dismissed contrary facts without consideration. Many government officials wanted segregated housing, and they held to their position regardless of the facts.

Following World War II, the federal government launched a concerted effort to help white Americans buy a house. This was the culmination of an idea that had been fomenting in Washington for decades.

While President, Woodrow Wilson grew increasingly concerned that the communist revolution that had overtaken Russia might soon come to America. He believed that the best way to prevent a similar revolution in America was for a large percentage of whites to own a house. His administration began touting the idea that whites had a patriotic duty to stop renting and buy a single-family house. The idea did not gain much traction until after World War II when several industries lobbied the federal government for political favors.

As with the banking industry, the construction and real estate industries had been decimated during the Depression. Construction permits decreased more than 90 percent from March 1928 to March 1933.[29] With the war over, leaders in banking, construction, and real estate began pressuring the federal government to enact policies that would revive their industries.

As a part of the GI Bill following the war, the Veteran's Administration (VA) began insuring (subsidizing) low-cost loans for veterans. But like the FHA, the VA would not insure loans for black veterans. Combined, the two agencies made it immensely easier for millions of whites to obtain a mortgage while denying that opportunity to non-white individuals. The result was a building boom. That boom occurred primarily in the suburbs where land was inexpensive. Low-cost loans and a greatly expanded and subsidized road system (the role that road subsidies have played in housing policy will be discussed in Chapter 7) fueled the boom. However, both zoning and government lending practices excluded non-whites from these opportunities simply because of skin color.

Government officials had long believed that home ownership is better than renting. The government then launched a series of programs to make home ownership easier for the preferred group. As with Low-Income Tax Credits, the government wanted Americans to take certain actions, and when individuals wouldn't or couldn't take those actions, the government bribed them with subsidized loans.

The government's efforts were effective in increasing home ownership rates. In 1940 about 45 percent of Americans owned their home. By 1956, that number had risen above 60 percent. However, blacks and other minorities did not enjoy the same opportunities to participate in this pursuit of the American dream. Ownership rates for whites were 20 percent higher than for blacks, and that disparity has grown wider in the years since. In early 2021, nearly 75 percent of whites owned their home compared to less than 45 percent of blacks.

For decades, the government's housing policies were explicitly intended to subsidize one group—whites—while denying the same benefits to non-white Americans. The government's racist lending policies made it much more difficult for many blacks to buy a home, build equity, and pass wealth to their children. Those policies have played a significant role in the wealth gap between whites and blacks. To be clear, there are many other factors that contribute to that wealth disparity, but in the past, racist government policies made it more difficult, though not impossible, for blacks to accumulate wealth. Government was playing favorites primarily on the basis of skin color, and there is no moral or just reason for government to do so.

In 1962, an executive order signed by President Kennedy prohibited racial discrimination in "the sale, leasing, rental, or other disposition of properties and facilities owned or operated by the federal government or provided with federal funds." The Fair Housing Act of 1968 expanded the prohibition to private actors. This didn't end the subsidies, it just increased the demand for them.

Subsidies For The "Underserved"

Since the late 1960s, in an effort to reverse past racist policies, Congress has passed a number of laws intended to increase home ownership among blacks and low-income families. One of the most significant was the Community Reinvestment Act in 1977. According to the website for the Federal Reserve, the act "requires the Federal Reserve and other federal banking regulators to *encourage* [emphasis added] financial institutions to help meet the credit needs of the communities in which they do business, including low- and moderate-income (LMI) neighborhoods."[30] However, the "encouragement" offered by banking regulators is actually a threat. Regulators require lenders to extend more credit to low- and moderate-income families or lose the government's permission to operate. This isn't encouragement. It is extortion.

In 1992, the Boston Federal Reserve (Fed) released a study that concluded that "even after controlling for financial, employment, and neighborhood characteristics, black and Hispanic mortgage applicants in the Boston metropolitan area are roughly 60 percent more likely to be turned down than whites."[31] As we have seen repeatedly, the focus of the study was on groups. But groups do not seek home mortgages, individuals do. And, as the study notes, "minority applicants, on average, do have greater debt burdens, higher loan-to-value ratios, and weaker credit histories and they are less likely to buy single-family homes than white applicants, and that these disadvantages do account for a large portion of the difference in denial rates."[32]

What is generally true of a group is seldom true of each member of that group. In general, minorities have greater debt burdens and weaker credit histories than whites, but this isn't true of every black or Hispanic. Nor is it true that every white has a low debt burden and a stellar credit history. When lenders look at an individual with more debt and a weak credit history, skin color is irrelevant. That individual is not a good credit risk, no matter his race or ethnicity.

Despite its flaws, the Fed's study quickly caught the attention of the banking industry, the civil rights community, the news media, and most significantly, bank regulators and Congress. Revisions to the Community Reinvestment Act occurred seven times from 1992 to 2008. Perhaps the most significant of these revisions were directives that the two government-sponsored enterprises (GSEs)—Fannie Mae and Freddie Mac—devote a percentage of their lending to support housing for low- and moderate-income families. This was set at 30 percent in 1992 and by 1999 it was up to 42 percent.

The Federal National Mortgage Association (Fannie Mae) was created by Congress in 1938. Fannie was created to purchase mortgages from local lenders and then packages those loans into a mortgage-backed security. This allows lenders to make more loans. For example, if a bank lends $100,000 for a house and one of the GSEs buys that mortgage, the bank recovers its money and can make another loan. By making more money available for mortgages, this is another way that government subsidies have been used to encourage Americans to buy a house.

In 1968, Congress split Fannie Mae into two separate entities—one private and one public. Fannie Mae became a private company, while the Government National Mortgage Association (Ginnie Mae) was created to guarantee the repayments of securities backed by mortgages made to government employees or veterans. The Federal Home Loan Mortgage Corporation (Freddie Mac) was created by Congress in 1970 to expand the secondary market for mortgages. Though the securities issued by the GSEs were not explicitly backed by the federal government, it was widely believed that the federal government would prevent a failure of the institutions. Indeed, this is precisely what happened during the financial crisis of 2007-08.

Neither GSE receives funds from the government. However, in 1996 the Congressional Budget Office noted, "But in the place of federal funds the government provides considerable unpriced benefits to the enterprises. Government-sponsored enterprises are costly to the government and taxpayers. The benefit is currently worth $6.5 billion annually."[33] These benefits give the GSEs an advantage over private lenders, and they now dominate the mortgage market.

The Creation Of A Crisis

In 1999, Housing and Urban Development Secretary Andrew Cuomo ordered the GSEs to increase their purchases of mortgages to low- and moderate-income families from 42 percent to 50 percent. Cuomo's policy required the GSEs to buy $2.4 trillion in mortgages over the next ten years to provide housing for 28.1 million low- and moderate-income families. Lending to minorities became, in the words of former BB&T President, John Allison, "a moral crusade for justice."[34] And that crusade was led by the GSEs.

For Cuomo's order to be met, lenders had to extend loans to individuals who had previously not qualified for a mortgage. As the 1992 Fed study noted, these individuals had "greater debt burdens, higher loan-to-value ratios, and weaker credit histories" than other borrowers—these were risky loans. A market for risky loans—subprime loans—had long existed, but it was a small percentage of mortgage lending. The new order from HUD meant a rapid expansion of that market.

In order to qualify these individuals for loans, lenders had to lower their standards. Former Fannie Mae CFO Timothy Howard writes that "the extreme relaxation in underwriting standards that began in the summer of 2003" led to the financial crisis in 2007-08.[35]

> Dramatically easier and widely available credit brought an avalanche of new buyers into the market who would not have been able to qualify for a mortgage under traditional underwriting, and by the time these buyers had pushed housing starts, home sales, and home prices to unsustainably high levels, there was nothing anyone could have done to prevent the ensuing collapse.[36]

With the GSEs buying the mortgages that private lenders originated, those lenders had no risk. Once the GSE bought a loan, the lender would not lose money if the loan went into default. This created an incentive to originate increasingly risky loans. Indeed, the only way the lenders could continue to make money was to write more and more loans. Lenders continued to lower their standards to the point that many were not even verifying income, which is a crucial factor in one's ability to repay a loan. The GSEs were complicit in the lowering of standards and continued to buy these risky mortgages. If the GSEs had refused to participate, the number of risky loans would have plummeted.

In addition to lowering standards, lenders also developed new mortgage products that made payments lower—at least for a while. One product was an adjustable-rate mortgage (ARM). Lenders often used a low initial interest rate to entice borrowers, and that rate, along with the monthly payment, could later be raised if interest rates increased. In 2004, 40 percent of all new mortgages were ARMs. Another product was "pick-a-payment" mortgages. Such loans allowed borrowers to pay less than the interest charges, which meant that the borrower's debt increased each month. That is not an effective strategy for building equity and wealth.

These subsidies resulted in home ownership climbing to an all-time high of 69 percent in 2004. Increased demand drove prices higher and higher. Many individuals found that they had substantial equity in their home. Many sold their home and then purchased a bigger and more expensive home. But the good times did not last. When interest rates began to go up, an increasing number of borrowers went into default. Home prices began to decline and many borrowers were underwater—they owed more on their home than it was worth.

In 2007-08 the housing bubble burst, and the financial markets suffered one of the worst crashes since the Great Depression. Many pundits and politicians have subsequently blamed the financial crisis on "predatory lenders" who took advantage of ill-informed borrowers. Undoubtedly, there were some lenders who were less than honest with their customers, but the entire housing bubble was only possible because of government policies. If the GSEs had not been buying the risky loans, lenders would not have written them. But if the GSEs had not purchased subprime loans, then traditionally underserved communities would have remained so. The GSEs incentivized bad behavior and made the subprime crisis possible. It is government policy, not "predatory lending," that is to blame.

Individual businesses often make bad decisions. However, the consequences of those choices are limited. When bad decisions permeate an industry, as it did in the financial industry during the 2000s, it is because of government policies. As John Allison writes, "Massive misinvestment requires government action."[37] In short, "Regulatory policies encourage [force] all lenders to make the same mistake."[38]

Public officials had long before declared that government must make home ownership easier for low-income families and minorities. But this policy failed to consider the fact that, for reasons that have nothing to do with race, some individuals are simply not good credit risks. This policy failed to consider the fact that home ownership involves much more than simply qualifying for a mortgage. A homeowner must not only service his debt, but must also pay for insurance, utilities, property taxes, and maintenance. An individual may be able to pay the mortgage, but a major expense, such as medical bills or home repairs, could be financially devastating if he doesn't have adequate funds available.

The government's policies regarding home ownership have focused on subsidizing specific groups—first whites and then minorities and low-income households. In the latter case, the result was a housing bubble. When the housing bubble burst, many of the intended beneficiaries of the government's subsidies suffered financially and lost their home.

Howard blames the Great Recession on regulators, writing that "U.S. financial regulators allowed, and indeed encouraged, the private-label mortgage-backed securities market to develop in a way that allowed its participants to profit from making loans their borrowers never could repay."[39] He conveniently ignores the fact that the GSEs were buying these loans.

For decades, the federal government enacted and implemented policies that explicitly excluded blacks and minorities from programs that aided white home buyers. Beginning in the late 1990s, government began a policy that is explicitly inclusionary—a policy aimed at helping blacks and other minorities. Inclusionary policies are simply the flip side of exclusionary policies. Both sides focus on the group. When the collective is the standard, individuals are harmed. And often, as the subprime loans illustrate, harm occurs even to the members of the favored group.

Subsidies Incentivize Destructive Behavior

The purpose of subsidies is to incentivize individuals to take actions that they would otherwise avoid. For example, if the monthly payment on a home mortgage is more than a household can afford, it won't buy the house. However, if government subsidizes that mortgage, the household can buy a house that was previously unaffordable. The household takes an action that it would have previously avoided. Certainly, subsidies can be beneficial to a household. However, subsidies can also be destructive because they arbitrarily increase demand for the subsidized value.

In the years leading up to the financial crisis of 2007-08, demand for housing increased significantly because of low interest rates and easy approval for mortgages. The increased demand drove prices up, and particularly for "starter homes" (lower priced homes that are more affordable for many first-time buyers). Many homeowners found that they had substantial equity in their starter home. They used that equity, along with the low interest rates being offered, to purchase a larger and more expensive house. This created more demand for the next tier of homes. As this process continued, prices at virtually every price level became unsustainable and millions of individuals ultimately suffered horrible financial losses when the bubble burst.

Subsidies incentivized destructive behavior. In the early 2000s, subsidies encouraged individuals to take on debt that they could not repay. In the short-term, they could afford the mortgage payment. But when their payment began to increase, they were in a difficult situation. Had the subsidies not existed, individuals would not have found themselves in that situation.

Subsidies also encouraged lenders to write very risky loans. With the potential for losing money virtually eliminated by the subsidies offered through the GSEs, lenders kept pouring more gasoline on the fire. Subsidies removed the risk faced by lenders, and so, they too engaged in behavior that was ultimately destructive to their businesses.

Without subsidies, neither borrowers nor lenders would have engaged in destructive behavior. Borrowers with poor credit would not have been able to obtain mortgages. Lenders would have more carefully assessed the risk of the loans they did consider. But the government wanted to encourage home ownership for low-income and minority households, and benefitting the group was the most important consideration.

Housing subsidies are founded on the Progressive framework. Whether government is subsidizing homeownership for whites or for low- and moderate-income households, the group serves as the standard. Policies are considered in isolation. In the early 2000s, subsidies increased homeownership for the favored group—low- and moderate income households—and any other consequences are dismissed or evaded until it was too late. At the same time, alternatives to the government's subsidy schemes became illegal. Lenders had to participate in the scheme if they wished to remain in business.

If we truly want to solve the housing crisis, then we must adopt a new framework. We must think about subsidies and homeownership in a fresh way.

MONETARY, TAX, AND FINANCIAL REGULATORY POLICIES

In Chapter 4 we saw how government uses prohibitions and mandates to compel individuals to act as the group demand. In Chapter 5, we saw how government uses subsidies to incentivize individuals to act as the group desires. In this chapter, we will examine how monetary and tax policies incentivize desired actions, while financial regulatory policies mandate desired actions. All of these policies have a profound impact on the availability and affordability of housing.

Like the previous policies that we have looked at, all of the policies examined in this chapter are founded on the Progressive framework. One group or another always serves as the standard. And these policies are always formulated and evaluated in isolation from other policies and issues.

This is not intended to be a comprehensive examination of these policies. The purpose here is to show how these policies impact housing.

Monetary Policy

Monetary policy is set by the Federal Reserve (the Fed). Created in 1913 to alleviate financial crises, the Fed was given three objectives: maximize employment, stabilize prices, and moderate long-term interest rates. The Fed uses monetary policy to pursue these objectives.

According to Investopedia, monetary policy "is a set of tools that a nation's central bank has available to promote sustainable economic growth by controlling the overall supply of money that is available to the nation's banks, its consumers, and its businesses."[40] The Fed has three ways that it controls the money supply—bank reserve requirements, interest rates, and open market operations.

Banks operate on a fractional reserve basis. They do not keep all of the deposits they receive as cash on hand. Instead, they loan most of that money to businesses and individuals. For example, if the reserve ratio is 10 percent, a bank that receives $1 million in deposits will retain only $100,000 and will loan the other $900,000. If the Fed raises the reserve requirement to 20 percent, the bank could only loan $800,000. Raising the reserve requirements will decrease the money available for lending, while lowering the reserve requirements will increase the money available for lending.

When the Fed wants to encourage spending, it lowers interest rates. It often does this to revive a sluggish economy, such as after the 9/11 terrorist attacks or the financial crisis of 2007-2008. When interest rates are low, the cost to borrowers is lower. Lower interest rates encourage individuals and businesses to buy new automobiles, homes, and other items bought on credit. The converse is also true. When the Fed wants to discourage spending—perhaps inflation is increasing— it raises interest rates. Higher interest rates reduce borrowing by both businesses and individuals.

The third method used by the Fed to increase the money supply is through open market operations. This occurs when the Fed creates new money and purchases securities, such as Treasury Notes or mortgage-backed securities, on the open market. This injects the new money into the economy. To illustrate, if the Fed buys $1 billion in securities, it uses money that previously did not exist and that money enters circulation to increase the money supply.

All of the Fed's policies ultimately have an impact on the affordability of housing, but interest rates have the most profound impact.   Lower interest rates make it less expensive to build and buy a home. Lower rates make it less expensive to build multi-family housing. Consequently, low interest rates generally increase the construction and sale of housing. Conversely, higher rates generally lead to reduced construction and sales.

Regarding single-family housing, interest rates can also impact the type of housing that is built and sold. The current interest rate will determine the amount of the mortgage that an individual can comfortably assume. And that, in turn, will determine the price of the house that he can buy.

As an example, consider a family that can afford a mortgage payment of $1,200 a month. Assuming an interest rate of 6 percent, the family could assume a $200,000 mortgage. However, if the interest rate was 4 percent, the family could afford the payments on a $250,000 mortgage. Lower interest rates not only enable more families to buy a home, but also a more expensive, and perhaps bigger, home. And this is precisely what happened in the 2000s.

In January 2001, the Fed began a series of cuts in interest rates. By July 2004, interest rates had dropped from 6 percent to 1 percent. This fueled a surge in home purchases in both the prime and subprime markets, but the growth in subprime loans was much greater. (Subprime mortgages are those made to individuals with poor credit scores—below 640.) In 2000, subprime loans accounted for about 10 percent of all mortgages. That number rose 25 percent in 2001, and then nearly doubled in 2003.[41]

The growth in subprime loans was a direct response to the directive issued by Housing and Urban Development Secretary Andrew Cuomo in 1999 that the government sponsored enterprises (GSEs)—Freddie Mac and Fannie Mae—

increase their subsidies to low- and moderate-income families. Many of these individuals had poor credit scores, and that fact had previously disqualified them from obtaining a mortgage. However, to meet Cuomo's order, the GSEs had to lower their standards. The GSEs dominated the mortgage market and bought a huge percentage of loans originated by other lenders. Following the lead of the GSEs, those lenders also lowered their standards.

The lenders who originated the loans devised several ways to qualify applicants. One of the most popular was an adjustable-rate mortgage (ARM). ARMs offered low down payments and low initial interest rates. However, if the Fed increased interest rates in the future, then the holder of an ARM could see a substantial increase in his monthly payment. As an example, on a $200,000 mortgage, an increase in the interest rate of 2 percent would increase the monthly payment by $230, or 27 percent. An interest rate increase of 3 percent would increase the payment by more than $350, or 42 percent.

With lowered standards, many families bought a home for the first time. The increased demand began to drive prices up. Families in starter homes suddenly had considerable equity and many sold their home to buy a bigger and more expensive home, which drove up prices in that market segment. As this process continued, home prices skyrocketed.

Then in June 2004 the Fed began raising interest rates. Two years later the rate was up to 5.24 percent and remained there for about a year. Monthly payments for those with ARMs increased substantially. At the same time, the increase in rates greatly slowed the home buying frenzy. With demand reduced, prices began to decrease. Suddenly, the good times of low interest rates, low monthly payments, and appreciating properties came to a screeching halt.

Many homeowners found that they now owed more than their house was worth. Many also discovered they were unable to afford the higher payments. Selling their home was difficult, and even if successful, many would have still owed money on it.

Many began to default and home prices declined further. As this process progressed, the economic devastation spread. In 2007 large financial companies began to declare bankruptcy and the entire financial system was threatened.

Two distinct government policies combined to cause the financial crisis of 2007-08. First, the Fed attempted to stimulate the economy by pumping money into the economy. Second, the order by HUD Secretary Cuomo to the GSEs provided an easy outlet for that money. The Fed was motivated by a desire to revive the economy for the benefit of "the public." Cuomo was motivated by a desire to advance a political agenda—greater home ownership for low- and moderate- income families. Both used the collective as the standard by which policies were evaluated.

Neither the Fed nor Cuomo anticipated how their policies would interact with one another. Each considered their policy in isolation. Though the policies were developed independently, they combined to create a housing bubble. When that bubble burst, millions were financially ruined, including many of those Cuomo had intended to benefit. The consequence of raising interest rates on families with ARMs was easy to predict. The consequences of making risky loans to low- and moderate-income families was also easy to predict. The combination of low interest rates and mandates to extend high-risk loans was financially toxic.

Both policies were intended to benefit some group. The Fed wanted to benefit "the public" by stimulating the economy. Cuomo wanted to benefit low- and moderate-income families. And because of the flawed Progressive framework—focusing on groups rather than individuals—the results were devasting to millions of individuals.

Cuomo's order was consistent with an idea long held by many government officials: home ownership is preferable to renting. Over the past eighty years, they have developed a variety of schemes to encourage and incentivize home ownership. One method that the government consistently uses is the tax code.

Tax Policies

Tax policy is frequently used to encourage or discourage certain types of action. For example, so-called "sin taxes" are often used to discourage the consumption of alcohol and cigarettes. Tax deductions and tax credits are used to encourage home ownership.

When the federal income tax was instituted in 1913, all interest payments were deductible. The Tax Reform Act of 1986 eliminated that deduction, except for mortgage interest. Lobbying from industry groups, particularly the National Association of Realtors (NAR), pressured Congress to retain the mortgage interest deduction. At the time, NAR claimed that any mention of reducing the tax benefits of home ownership could endanger property values. NAR repeated this position in 2010 after the Debt Reduction Task Force recommended reducing the interest deduction, saying that the organization would "remain vigilant in opposing any plan that modifies or excludes the deductibility of mortgage interest."[42]

Another industry group, the National Association of Home Builders (NAHB) agrees that the tax code should encourage home ownership. However, NAHB believes that a tax credit would better serve that purpose. In June 2021, NAHB CEO Jerry Howard told Congress,

> A shift away from the mortgage interest deduction to a permanent homeownership tax credit that is targeted to lower- and middle-income Americans would make homeownership more accessible to hardworking American families. Additionally, a permanent, first-time home buyer tax credit would complement this shift and could provide some relief to the challenge of accumulating a down payment.[43]

Both NAR and NAHB are politically influential organizations. Both contribute millions annually to candidates and they spend even more on lobbying efforts. In 2020 alone, NAR contributed $14 million to candidates and spent $84 million on lobbying. That same year, NAHB donated $2.9 million and spent $3.6 million on lobbying. Though they disagree on the particular benefits that homeowners should receive, they agree that tax policy should favor a particular group—homeowners. While the influence that tax policy has on home ownership is impossible to measure, the fact that two national organizations related to housing favor such tax benefits makes it clear that they think it helps their industries.

The mortgage interest deduction is only one of the tax benefits extended to homeowners. Property taxes are also deductible. And the purchase of certain energy saving equipment, such as solar panels, can earn tax credits. In the latter case, the credit is an explicit attempt to incentivize homeowner investment in "renewable" energy, an action that many would not take without tax benefits.

These deductions and credits are all designed to influence the actions of individuals. Government officials want Americans to own a home, and so they have created a multitude of programs and policies to encourage and entice to us act in the desired way. Nothing we buy receives the level of tax benefits and subsidies as the purchase of a home.

Tax credits are also used to incentivize the construction of below-market rental housing. The Low-Income Housing Tax Credit (LIHTC) provides developers with credits for building housing for low-and moderate-income families. The tax credits are intended to offset the lost revenue from offering some units below market rates. Developers usually sell the credits to investors to raise funds for construction. The investors then use the credits to offset their income.

The tax credits are distributed by HUD to the individual states, and state agencies then distribute the credits to developers. The program currently allocates about $8 billion per year for the construction of about 106,000 units.

Like all tax credits, LIHTC is used to incentivize actions

that individuals otherwise would not take. In the case of low-income housing, developers would not offer units at a loss, and market rates would price low- and moderate-income families out of many developments. The LIHTC is essentially a bribe to developers to lower the rents they charge a certain group of people.

In this chapter we have looked at policies intended to encourage or incentivize desired actions. Because these types of policies incentivize rather than mandate, they allow individuals to make choices and act on them. However, there are other policies that eliminate such choices.

Regulatory Policies

Banking regulations establish what banks can do and what they must do. These policies can have a significant impact on housing. Former banker John Allision notes,

> Individual market participants are always making mistakes. However, not all competitors make the same mistake, and different parties often make counterbalancing mistakes unless "Big Brother," in this case the Federal Reserve, drives almost all market participants in the same wrong direction.[44]

This is what occurred in the 1990s and 2000s. Government regulatory policies, in combination with lower interest rates and HUD's directive for the government-sponsored enterprises, were behind a massive misallocation of capital. Regulatory policies forced all mortgage lenders to make the same mistake—extend loans to high-risk borrowers.

On the federal level, there are at least six different agencies that regulate banks and credit unions. These agencies impose a morass of restrictions and mandates on lenders. Top banking executives spend an inordinate amount of time simply trying to satisfy regulators. The failure to do so can result in significant penalties, including revocation of the bank's charter.

Satisfying regulators is a matter of survival. One example is the Community Reinvestment Act (CRA).

The CRA was first enacted in 1977 and subsequently revised at least nine times. The stated purpose of the act was to combat previous racism in lending by requiring banks to extend a certain percentage of their loans in low- and moderate-income neighborhoods.

Banks are regularly audited and rated on their adherence to the dictates of the CRA. "In order to make acquisitions, open branches, and generally grow its business, a bank must have a satisfactory CRA rating," writes Allison.[45] He goes on to state that the law requires banks to engage in destructive behavior: "It was explicitly clear that under the act, banks had a legal duty to make high-risk home loans to low-income borrowers."[46] This was a recipe for disaster, and it was forced upon banks by Congress in an attempt to overcome past racism in housing.

While Congress, regulators, and pundits have blamed private businesses for racist lending and housing policies, those actions were driven by government policies and mandates. Governments used zoning to exclude blacks from many neighborhoods. For decades, two agencies of the federal government—the Federal Housing Administration and the Veterans Administration—refused to provide mortgages for blacks. State licensing boards prohibited realtors from selling homes in predominantly white neighborhoods to blacks.

These unjust laws and policies should have never existed in a nation dedicated to the proposition that all individuals are created equal and endowed with certain unalienable rights. The repeal of these laws, though often too long in coming, was a step towards protecting the rights of all individuals. Repealing those laws was a step towards housing justice. Repealing those laws was a step towards protecting the freedom of all individuals to produce or earn the housing that they desire.

But many were not and are not satisfied with simply repealing immoral laws. They believe that some form of restitution must be paid to the victims of those laws. And that has served as a part of the motivation for the CRA, as well as subsequent amendments. This might seem like the just thing to do. But we cannot evaluate this issue, or any issue, without considering the full context.

To begin, neither the victims nor the actual responsible parties are easy to identify. Instead, we are told to look at the issue from the perspective of groups. Because many individual blacks were victims of government racism, the argument goes, then we must act as if all blacks were victims. Because many whites supported and implemented policies of racial discrimination, then we must act as if all whites were guilty of racism.

Even if something is true of a large percentage of the members of a group, it is seldom true of every member of that group. Many blacks were not victims of racism regarding zoning or home mortgages. Many whites did not support or implement racist policies.

Justice demands that the guilty be punished and they make restitution to the victim. To give restitution to those who were not victims is to grant unearned rewards. To punish those who did not participate in an injustice is to penalize the innocent. Neither is an act of justice. Neither restitution nor punishment should be dispensed simply because of skin color. Yet, this was what the CRA and similar programs essentially do.

An example of the proper way to pursue justice is "Bruce's Beach." In 1912, Willa and Charles Bruce bought land in Manhattan Beach, a suburb of Los Angeles on the Pacific Ocean. They built a resort that catered to blacks, who were prohibited from other beaches. The resort flourished until the 1920s, when the city used eminent domain to seize the land for a park. The park was never built, and the land sat vacant for decades. Ownership was transferred to the state in 1948. In 2021, the land was returned to the Bruce family. In this instance, the victim could be identified, and restitution was made by the guilty party—the government.

Forcing banks to extend loans to minority and high-risk

borrowers reduces the money available for loans to less risky borrowers of all races and ethnicities. The CRA gives those with poor credit scores a benefit at the expense of those with better scores. To meet the demands of the CRA, a high-risk borrower has an equal, and perhaps better, chance to obtain a mortgage as an individual who is less risky. This is not justice. It is an attempt to correct one injustice with another injustice, and that is a gross contradiction. The defenders of CRA aren't concerned with the individuals who are victimized by its requirements.

Rational lenders do not care about a borrower's race or ethnicity. They care about his ability to repay the loan, and factors such as one's credit history and credit score provide some measure of a borrower's riskiness. But the CRA requires bankers to ignore rational criteria and give more weight to skin color.

As we've previously seen, this required lending standards to be lowered. And because the government-sponsored enterprises dominated the mortgage market and were buying many subprime loans, originators had little concern about a borrower's ability to repay the loan. They made money by writing loans, and after that, collection was someone else's problem. This irresponsible behavior was made possible by, and in the case of the CRA, mandated by government policies.

In the aftermath of the financial crisis of 2007-08, many accused banks and mortgage companies of "predatory lending." These institutions, the claim goes, took advantage of uninformed individuals in the pursuit of profits. It is true that lenders were trying to make a profit, but they would not have written risky loans to low-income borrowers if they had not been forced to. The CRA required them to do so, and the GSEs made it possible for them to make a profit writing worthless loans. Congress, HUD, and the GSEs were not the only culprits.

One of the government agencies that regulates banks is the Security and Exchange Commission (SEC), which was created in 1934 with a "mission of protecting investors, maintaining fair, orderly, and efficient markets, and facilitating capital formation."[47] In the early 2000s, the SEC required banks to change how they evaluate loans and calculate what they should hold in reserve for bad loans. John Allison explains, "The SEC forced the banking industry to remove judgment based on experience from the loan loss reserve decision and to create a process that is almost exclusively mathematically based. This change caused banks to reduce their loan loss reserves substantially."[48]

Though banks try to only extend loans to those who will repay, they know that some borrowers will eventually default. To mitigate the financial damage, they hold some funds in reserve. If a loan goes into default, the bank can draw on the loan loss reserve to help recover from the loss.

Reducing loan loss reserves can work, but only if the default rate is low. But if many borrowers default, the reserve can be depleted rapidly. And this is what happened in 2007. As the number of loans in default grew, banks began running out of funds to continue operations. This catastrophe was not the consequence of individual banks making bad choices. It was a result of the SEC's mandate to lower loan loss reserves and the CRA's mandate to extend risky loans. One government policy forced banks to make loans that had a high likelihood of going into default, while another policy prohibited banks from holding sufficient funds to offset bad loans.

Despite its mission to protect investors, the SEC failed horribly in the 2000s. It did nothing about the mortgage-backed securities being created by the GSEs, allowing Fannie Mae and Freddie Mac to continue bundling worthless mortgages into worthless securities. Those "securities" were secure as quicksand, yet the SEC allowed these toxic financial instruments to proliferate. The second failure to rock the SEC in the 2000s was Bernie Madoff. Though he had been reporting to the SEC for decades, the agency never found a problem with his $50 billion Ponzi scheme.

Many have argued that the agency's lack of enforcement is because of "revolving door" mentality. Many staff members of the SEC work at the agency for a few years, develop connections, and then enter the private sector to use their connections for the benefit of their new employer. As a result, staff members are reluctant to vigorously enforce regulations—it's a case of not biting the hand that might feed you in the future. Undoubtedly, there is an element of truth in that. However, that isn't the fundamental issue.

The point here isn't whether the SEC should have done a better job. The point is, the SEC should have never been created. The SEC, as well as many similar agencies, creates a false sense of security. In the case of the SEC, many investors assume that the agency's stamp of approval (or lack of citations) means that a company or security is safe. And so, investors often trust the regulatory agency and fail to do their own due diligence. But both the financial crisis and Bernie Madoff make it clear that the SEC isn't protecting investors. Instead, in the case of loan loss reserves, when it issues a mandate all market participants must follow, the entire industry can be lead over the cliff.

Push And Pull

Regulations and mandates push lenders, individuals, and businesses into certain actions, i.e., force us to act a desired way. Tax credits and monetary policies pull banks, individuals, and businesses into certain actions, i.e., incentivize us to act in a desired way. Whether they are pushing or pulling, public officials are constantly trying to plan and control the actions of individuals and businesses for the alleged benefit of one group or another.

Underlying these policies is the desire to poke, prod, and cajole everyone to do the "right" things. And the right thing is whatever bureaucrats and politicians declare it to be. This presumes that a certain course of action is right for everyone, and government officials know what it is. Success is measured by the number of people who conform.

However, Americans are not monolithic regarding desires and values. We seek a wide range of values. Some like baseball and others like ballet. Some like Jay Z and some prefer Mozart. Some enjoy parks while others enjoy the mall. We want different things in life. Public officials find this problematic because some of us choose a course of action that those officials find objectionable. And so, they seek to prevent us from acting as we think best by mandating, prohibiting, and incentivizing.

Such an approach treats us like children who can't be trusted to make rational decisions. Rather than protect our freedom to live as autonomous, independent individuals, these policies make us dependent.

These policies are founded on the same Progressive framework as zoning and housing subsidies. Each regards the group as the standard. Each of these policies are developed and analyzed in isolation. The immediate benefits to the favored group is the only consideration. Alternatives are dismissed or evaded. We must reject this framework of seeking benefits for one group or another. Instead, we must embrace a framework that enables all individuals to flourish.

HIGHWAY POLICY

For most of the policies that we have examined so far, the connection to housing is generally obvious. However, the relationship between housing and one set of policies is not as evident. Despite this, federal highway policy has arguably done more to shape where Americans live than any other set of policies.

Like many of the other policies and institutions that we have examined, federal involvement in highways began during the Progressive Era and its aftermath. This was a time when the public began to demand that government expand its powers and rely on "experts" to provide guidance on the proper policies. Roads and highways were one such issue. The results of these policies are with us still today: urban sprawl, the destruction of mass transportation, and the loss of countless affordable homes.

The Good Roads Movement

At the end of the 19th century, roads were primarily a state or local issue. The federal government's involvement in roads was limited to "post roads"—roads used to transport mail between major cities. The quality of most roads, particularly outside of large cities, was poor. But we must remember that, at the time, the primary modes of transportation were walking, horses, and increasingly, bicycles.

Though the bicycle had been invented in 1817, it did not become popular in the United States until the last two decades of the 19th century. The bicycle offered an easy way to move from one place to another, and it did not require the care necessary for horses. Suffragette Susan B. Anthony once remarked that cycling "has done more to emancipate women than anything else in the world. It gives women a feeling of freedom and self-reliance. I stand and rejoice every time I see a woman ride by on a wheel... the picture of free, untrammeled womanhood."

As cycling became more popular, a coalition of bicycle enthusiasts began to promote the need for better roads and highways. Called the Good Roads movement, they asserted that better roads would be a public good, and therefore, government should become more involved. Framing the issue in this manner allowed them to promote their own self-interests under the guise of promoting the well-being of the group—"the public."

Funded primarily by Albert Pope, a leading manufacturer of bicycles, the leaders of the movement wrote and distributed books and pamphlets. They focused their efforts on farmers, who were already an influential political constituency. The movement tried to convince farmers that better roads would make transportation to markets easier. However, farmers were generally disinterested, believing that they would be taxed for the new roads. Initially, the main support for the movement came from bicyclists.

Under pressure from the Good Roads movement, in 1893 the federal government established the Office for Road Inquiry (ORI) to study the feasibility of a system of public roads. General Roy Stone, a Civil War hero, civil engineer, and one of the leaders of the Good Roads movement was picked to head the office. Over the next few years Stone and his small staff wrote technical and promotional materials, and Stone was a frequent and popular speaker at Good Roads conventions. He also helped draft model bills for state legislators seeking to improve roads. Though he had little actual experience in road construction, Stone was regarded as an expert on the subject.

As Owen D. Gutfreund writes in *Twentieth-Century Sprawl: Highways and the Reshaping of the American Landscape,*

Since this was an age characterized by a great deal of confidence in the ability of "experts," the findings of the engineers employed by the ORI (and its successor agencies) were not questioned. The public officials charged with evaluating and formulating new state highway policies were usually drawn from the ranks of the Good Roads movement and therefore approached the issues with the predisposed notion of providing new roads as a free-of-charge public good.[49]

Beginning in 1896, Stone also worked with the postal service to establish Rural Free Delivery (RFD), a program that demonstrated to farmers the benefits of good roads. When farmers realized that they wouldn't be taxed to pay for new roads, they quickly joined the movement. In 1911, Congress began making grants for road construction to expand the RFD program. The nature of the program meant the funds were to be used only in rural areas, rather than in the nation's cities. By this time, the popularity of bicycles was waning, being replaced by the automobile.

The growth in automobile use brought new industries into the Good Roads movement. Automobile and parts manufacturers, hotels, gas stations, repair garages, and real estate developers all began promoting the need for better roads. The movement had effectively framed highways as a public good, and there was little debate over whether the federal government would become involved. The only question was: how would it be involved? That question was answered in 1916 with the passage of the Federal Aid Road Act.

The act authorized $75 million over a five-year period. The money would be distributed to state highway departments, which would pay for half of the construction costs. Since most states did not have a highway department at the time, they began scrambling to create such departments so that they could qualify for the federal grants. The act also stipulated that the money could only be used for rural post roads.

Following the dominant framework of the time, construction of the roads was considered in isolation from other issues, most notably, how to pay for the roads. The act imposed no user fees on motorists, and attempts to impose a national tax on gasoline were defeated by the lobbying efforts of automobile groups, oil companies, and other related industries. Requiring the users of the new roads to pay for those roads was counter to the Good Roads movement's call for free highways —freeways. The result was an enormous government subsidy for automobile use, and the provisions of the act directed these subsidies entirely to rural areas. "In effect," writes Gudfreund,

> the federal government established a system of transfer payments, from urbanized regions to rural regions, and from all taxpayers to those who drove automobiles. In 1921 users of the 9 million motor vehicles in the nation paid only twelve percent of all highway costs. In the mid-1920s, $1.5 billion went into new construction of roads and highways each year, while user fees collected at all levels of government were only $472 million.[50]

In short, the nation's highways were subsidized from the beginning. And it was driven by the Progressive framework that holds the group as the standard of value.

Each proposal for higher user fees, tolls, or other measures to charge auto users the full cost of the roads was quickly defeated. Road advocates argued "it would be unfair for motorists to pay the full cost of highways because they conferred a 'general benefit' and therefore should be funded out of general revenues."[51] The result was an increased demand for highways, and that demand continues to this day.

That most people derive a benefit from something does not justify taxing them for its provision. We all benefit from air transport because, but that doesn't mean that we should be taxed to pay for plane fares. However, given the dominance of the Progressive framework, this was an effective way to frame discussions of road policy.

The Birth Of The Suburbs

The focus on rural roads meant that state highway departments could do little inside urbanized areas. Outside of the cities, roads were improving rapidly and dramatically. Real estate developers were quick to see the opportunities that the new freeways provided. They began building industrial parks, strip centers, and residential subdivisions near the freeways. And government planners not only accepted the growing dependency on automobiles, they embraced the idea that government should meet the growing demands for more roads without question and without directly charging motorists.

The result was a migration of residents and businesses from the inner city to the suburbs, and with it, greater dependency on the automobile. The migration began slowly, but after World War II it accelerated dramatically. That migration was aided by General Motors famous Futurama exhibit at the 1939 World's Fair in New York City. Many of the documentaries shown at the fair promoted slum clearance, planned "satellite" towns, and decentralization. It was

> a superbly effective manifesto for anti-urban city planning, centered around an outright rejection of existing urbanization patterns in favor of new-construction suburban subdivision in the garden-city tradition, beyond the limits of existing metropolitan areas, linked to other settlements by newly built highways.[52]

As we saw previously, after World War II both the Federal Housing Administration and the Veterans Administration were offering inexpensive mortgages. As we also saw, blacks were excluded from obtaining these loans. The result was "white-flight"—a mass movement of whites from the city to the suburbs.

The new freeways made it easy for them to commute to the city for work or entertainment, and they did not have to bear the full cost of their transportation. The lower land values in the suburbs and government subsidies made it inexpensive to buy a home. The suburbs became predominantly white as middle-class whites abandoned the cities to low-income whites and blacks.

Suburban governments were quick to use exclusionary zoning to keep "undesirables" out of their neighborhoods. Single-family zoning prohibited multi-family housing and other forms of less expensive housing. The combination of low-cost government loans to whites and single-family zoning virtually guaranteed that the suburbs would become economically and racially segregated.

This flight to the suburbs had a devasting impact on the cities. The cities' tax bases were declining significantly. In response, poorer neighborhoods—predominantly black—were neglected, while the remaining wealthier neighborhoods—predominantly white—had better streets, schools, and parks.

The post-war years also witnessed an increased interest in "urban renewal," initially on the local level. These efforts were guided by city public housing agencies, which demolished slums and built replacement affordable housing. But in the mid-1950s, urban renewal took on an entirely different meaning with the passage of the Federal Aid Highway Act of 1956.

The Interstate Highway System

Considered the hallmark of the Eisenhower administration, the interstate highway system was created by the Federal Aid Highway Act of 1956. General Lucius D. Clay lead a committee that was given the task of developing an interstate highway system plan. Reminiscent of the Good Roads movement, Clay said, "It was evident we needed better highways. We needed them for safety, to accommodate more automobiles. We needed them for defense purposes, if that should ever be necessary. And we needed them for the economy. Not just as a public works measure, but for future growth."[53] In short, the interstate highway system would benefit the group—"the public."

Clay proposed a $100 billion program to build 40,000 miles of highway in ten years. The system would link every American city with a population of more than 50,000. Eisenhower wanted the system to be funded by tolls, but Clay convinced him that tolls were only feasible in more heavily populated areas, such as the northeast. Construction would be funded by a federal gasoline tax, thereby shifting some of the cost to users of the new highways. The federal government would pay 90 percent of the construction costs with the states paying the remaining costs. Each state would own the portion of the highways running within its borders.

The nature of the project meant that much of the system would be built in rural areas. Though this required the use of eminent domain to seize private property, few homes or businesses were involved. However, in urban areas, the story was much different.

Building a four-lane highway through densely populated areas required the seizure and demolition of hundreds of thousands of homes and businesses. And the victims of this destruction were predominantly low-income minorities. Wealthier individuals had the political influence to fight plans to route the new highways through or near their neighborhoods.

Construction resulted in the demolition of entire neighborhoods, but governments did virtually nothing to help those whose homes had been seized and demolished. As Richard Rothstein notes in *The Color of Law,*

> When enacted into law in 1956, the interstate highway program did not impose even a nominal obligation on federal or state governments to assist those whose residences were being demolished. Although the House version of the bill permitted (but did not require) payment of moving costs to tenants in demolished homes, the Eisenhower administration objected. Council of Economic Advisors chairman Arthur Burns warned

that compensation would "run up the cost" of the highway program, predicting that the system would evict nearly 100,000 people a year as it grew.[54]

"The public" got the benefit of an expanded freeway system, while low-income individuals and minorities lost their homes and businesses. The group allegedly benefitted while hundreds of thousands of individuals suffered. When the collective is the standard, what happens to individuals is regarded as irrelevant.

City planners soon saw the interstate system as a way to address "blighted" areas. "The funds were seen as a way to fix the urban core by replacing blight with freeways," says Joseph DiMento, co-author of *Changing Lanes: Visions and Histories of Urban Freeways*.[55] The process was dominated by highway engineers. "They were trained to design without consideration for how a highway might impact urban fabric," DiMento added, "they were worried about the most efficient way of moving people from A to B."[56]

And so, while federal highway policies subsidized the transportation of middle-class suburbanites, those same policies were destroying the homes of low-income residents of the city. Highway policies truly shaped the American landscape.

This isn't merely a story from history. It continues to this day, with government spending hundreds of billions of dollars each year repairing and expanding highways. And when necessary, government continues to seize and demolish homes. One recent example can be found near Charleston, South Carolina.

In the late 1950s, Liberty Park and Highland Terrace were vibrant, predominantly black neighborhoods. But then, in 1969 a freeway divided the two neighborhoods and demolished homes, businesses, and churches. Today, the state wants to widen a highway interchange near the neighborhoods. Nearly three dozen single-family homes, four apartment buildings, eleven mobile homes, eight duplexes, two community centers, and at least one church will be seized and demolished to make way for the freeway expansion. At a time when a housing shortage exists in most cities—including Charleston—the state wants to wipe out nearly one-hundred homes. This is what happens when policies are formulated by using the group— in this case "the public"—as the standard to evaluate a policy. When the group is the standard, individual human beings are victimized.

In the late 19th and early 20th centuries, the Good Roads movement promoted the idea that highways and roads should be free for motorists to use and provided by government. Alternatives weren't discussed or seriously considered. Gutfreund writes,

> There was never any sustained effort to offer a differing perspective. Highway policy discussions were generally framed as questions of efficient service delivery and were initially dominated almost exclusively by engineers. The narrowly conceived public debates obscured the powerful effect of the resultant subsidies on American communities of all shapes and sizes. The terms of the discourse and the main policy precedents were firmly established by mid-century, at which point they were set in concrete, literally, by the Interstate Highway legislation.[57]

One of the consequences of this framework is urban sprawl. The resulting traffic congestion angers commuters, who demand that more money be spent on freeways. This was a result that could have been predicted if the full context had been examined.

Economists have long noted that if something is subsidized, we get more of it, and that is what has happened to freeway use. When users to not have to pay the full cost for something, they will use it more because they have no motivation to economize their automobile use or find alternative transportation.

Another, more tragic, consequence is the destruction of hundreds of thousands of affordable homes. When the alleged interests of the group are supreme, individual lives are ruined.

By now, it should be clear that government policies have

directly caused our current housing crisis. Single-family zoning has made housing density illegal in much of the country. Government backed mortgages have expanded the demand for home ownership beyond its natural level, causing prices to continually rise. Monetary and tax policies further encourage home ownership and put upward pressure on housing prices. Highway policies have subsidized suburban living at the expense of urban residents.

Shaping The American Landscape

For more than a century, road and highway policies, combined with other government policies, have dramatically reshaped the American landscape. Density was discouraged, and often outlawed. Dependency on the automobile destroyed a once-thriving mass transit system in most cities. Instead of allowing cities to grow naturally and organically, highway policy arbitrarily and abruptly shifted the population from the cities to the suburbs.

The framework for highway policies, like nearly all of the policies examined so far, were first formed during the Progressive Era. The Progressive framework has been retained throughout the years since, and it has contributed to our current housing crisis.

Highway policy has not been intended to mandate, prohibit, or incentivize desired actions. However, it was and remains founded on the same framework as other policies that we have examined. Policies are evaluated solely on the basis of perceived benefits to the group. The policies were and are evaluated out of context, and alternatives are rarely considered. If we truly want to solve the housing crisis, then we must reject this framework. And we must do so, not just regarding housing policies, but every policy founded on this flawed framework. We need fresh thinking about highway policy.

PERSONAL CHOICE AND THE FREEDOM TO EARN A LIVING

Much has been written about the impact landlords, developers, gentrifiers, and other housing producers have on the affordability of housing. But scant attention has been paid to two other relevant topics.

The affordability of housing involves more than just the price of housing. One's income determines what is affordable, as well as one's housing options. We are frequently told that someone making minimum wage cannot afford a two-bedroom apartment in most cities. We aren't told why an individual is making minimum wage or why he needs a two-bedroom apartment.

One's income is a function of one's production. An individual who produces more values is generally paid more than a less productive individual. And an individual's ability to produce values is determined by his skills, experience, and knowledge. No matter where one begins in life, one can always gain new and better skills, experience, and knowledge to increase one's productive abilities, i.e., increase one's income.

Each of us faces the option of stagnating or improving our capacities. We each have the choice to learn and grow or plod along in passive acceptance of our current situation. We each have the ability to increase our income. Whether we exercise that ability or not is a choice each of us makes, whether consciously and explicitly or not.

We cannot examine the affordability of housing without taking personal choice into account. Yet, housing advocates seldom address the issue. They tell us stories of families struggling to stay housed, and then blame greedy landlords. They ignore the role that personal choice plays in the equation. They fail to consider the full context.

Similarly, housing advocates do not address impediments to earning a living. Minimum wage laws, occupational licensing, and pro-union laws limit opportunities and earning potential. These laws often prevent individuals from obtaining job skills and experience. These restrictions must also be examined if we are to consider the full context regarding housing affordability.

Personal Choice

Just as we must adopt the proper framework for evaluating public policies, we must adopt the proper framework for evaluating the myriad personal choices that we face each day. The choices that we make today determine the opportunities available to us tomorrow. The choices that we make today can open doors or close doors. If we make good choices, then we are much more likely to attain the values that we seek. And if we make bad choices, then we are unlikely to attain the values that we seek. Our framework will determine how we evaluate the choices that confront us, and in turn, our success or failure in the pursuit of values.

We cannot consider either our ends or the means out of context or in isolation. If our goal is clear, then we must consider all of the related issues, including how we will obtain the desired value. For example, if we decide that the way to increase our income is to take night classes, we have to consider the time and expense that this will entail.

We must also consider the pros and cons of each alternative. Rather than attend night classes, perhaps a second job will provide an opportunity to learn new skills. But this requires consideration of which skills to learn, as well as how this would impact other areas of our life. All of this requires us to think long-term rather than range of the moment. We must identify how each alternative will affect us, not just today, but next week, next month, next year. A personal story provides both a positive and a negative example of this point.

At the age of sixteen, I decided that I wanted to be a journalist. However, after discussing this with counselors and visiting several colleges, I concluded that the job prospects weren't good for journalists. So, I abandoned that goal to pursue an associate degree in electronics. Looking back, I made the decision hastily and without considering the full context or alternatives. I looked at the issue from one perspective—the immediate job prospects. In my out of context thinking, I didn't realize that journalism isn't the only way to make a living by writing. Nor did I consider the possibility that, despite the discouraging job prospects, I may have still found a job as a journalist. In short, I approached the issue with the wrong framework. This doesn't mean that I regret my choices. However, if I had employed the proper framework, I might have made a different decision.

By my mid-twenties I was doing research and development for an oil services company. The job paid well, and I enjoyed it. But then two things happened in a relatively short period of time, and I began to wonder if I would be happy remaining at that job. First, management changes were making the job less enjoyable. Second, I witnessed several co-workers go through a mid-life crisis.

I couldn't do much about the management changes other than complain, and that wasn't very effective. However, I gave a lot of thought to the issue of mid-life crisis. Each of the co-workers had married young and had children. Each divorced their wife about fifteen years later and took up with a much younger woman. Based on what they said to me, as well as what I observed, I began to understand the cause of their mid-life crisis. By marrying and having children at a young age, they gave up some of their dreams to fulfill their parental responsibilities. And then years later, they felt remorse. They responded by trying to regain their youth or something resembling it. I vowed that that would not happen to me. I decided that I would try to make a living as a free-lance writer.

Unlike my decision to abandon writing as a teenager, this decision was reached after careful consideration for months. I realized that I would struggle at first, perhaps for years. And so, I developed a fifteen-month plan. I decided to stay in my job and live very frugally so that I could save as much as possible. I began writing in the evening and on weekends to hone my skills. My decision to quit my job was much better informed than my decision to not attend journalism school. In this situation, I did consider the full context, as well as alternatives.

When I quit my job, I had saved enough to live for about two years, which I thought was a reasonable amount of time to establish myself. I also decided that if I was unable to support myself by writing, I would get a part-time job. I had a plan and a backup plan. In making this decision, I was thinking long-term.

In both of these situations the choices that I made determined the opportunities available in the future. The choices I made as a teenager limited my immediate opportunities for writing. As a young adult, my choices opened up new opportunities. The same is true for every individual.

Starting at a young age, we all make choices that have long-term impacts, though we often do not realize that at the time. If we goof off in school and don't apply ourselves, we close doors to future opportunities. If our English and communication skills are lacking, we will have fewer employment options. If we are a lazy employee, we won't advance and may get fired. In regard to each of these, we have a choice regarding the path that we will follow. And at any point along the way, we can change the path that we are on by making better choices.

These facts are usually evaded by housing advocates. When they share the stories of low-income families, they don't mention why the family has a low income. They say nothing of the choices these individuals have made and are making. They fail to consider the fact that poor choices may be the reason that the family is poor.

Consider the story of Doreen that Matthew Desmond tells in *Evicted: Poverty and Profit in the American City*. Doreen was a single mother with four children. When she discovered that her teenage daughter was pregnant, she was thrilled. Though she was facing eviction for being behind on her rent, Doreen welcomed another mouth to feed. Doreen's older daughter, herself a single mother, told her pregnant sister, "We didn't have a daddy. My kids don't have no daddy. And your kids don't need no daddy."[58] Unable to properly provide for the children they already had, this family continued to choose to have children and add to their financial burden. It is no wonder that they struggled to stay housed.

Or consider the story of Larraine from the same book. After receiving her food stamps one month, she spent the entire amount for a single meal of lobster, shrimp, king crab legs, and pie. A pastor who helped Larraine on occasion thought that many of her problems were self-inflicted. He said, "She made some stupid choices, spending her money foolishly....Making her go without for a while may be the best thing for her, so that she can be reminded, 'Hey when I make foolish choices there are consequences.'"[59]

Choices do have consequences. If we are going to address housing affordability, we must acknowledge the role that personal choice plays. To do otherwise is to pretend that personal choices have no impact on one's income or one's ability to afford housing, and that means dropping the context.

This does not mean that we should be callous towards those who make poor choices. But we do them no favors by excusing and enabling poor choices. If we subsidize irresponsibility, if we excuse poor decisions, we will get more of it. Instead, we must hold individuals accountable for their choices and counsel them to make better choices in the future.

Unfortunately, many people who do make good choices face arbitrary barriers that limit their freedom to earn a living. One of the most significant is the minimum wage.

Minimum Wage Laws Harm Low-Skilled Workers

The federal minimum wage was first established by the Fair Labor Standards Act in 1938. This is another Progressive Era policy that continues to haunt us today. From the initial twenty-five cents per hour, the minimum wage has been raised twenty times to reach its current $7.25. Many states and cities have a higher minimum wage.

Minimum wage laws prohibit employers from paying what many low-skilled jobs are worth. But more significantly, such laws prohibit low-skilled workers from accepting a low wage in order to obtain job skills and experience. Rather than a low wage, they get no wage. Rather than gain valuable experience, they are left jobless and unskilled.

A low-skilled worker has little productive capacity other than ambition and conscientiousness. But if he is unable to secure a job, his ambition and conscientiousness cannot be demonstrated. If he is unable to obtain a job, he cannot develop his capacity. He will remain a low- or unskilled worker.

To illustrate, consider a teenager who has never worked before. He lives at home, so his expenses are minimal. He doesn't need a high wage. In his context, what he needs is experience, and he may be willing to work for $5 an hour to obtain that experience. And if he is ambitious and conscientious, a rational employer will quickly give him a raise if the employee is worth it. Minimum wage laws deny opportunities to low-skilled workers and make it harder for businesses to offer those opportunities. Minimum wage laws prevent both employers and employees from agreeing to a wage that both find acceptable. This is an injustice to both.

Defenders of minimum wage argue that it is impossible to support a family on $7.25 an hour. This is true, but it illustrates my earlier point. An individual who is earning minimum wage might be better served delaying parenthood until he is able to support children. And if he chooses to have children, then he must accept the fact that the costs will greatly reduce his housing options.

Some housing advocates claim that this is racist and classist. Jennifer Bennetech, the founder of Occupy Philadelphia, wrote, that "the focus on 'smart growth' and density makes it more difficult for low-income people to have large families. Essentially, it sends a message that problematizes the choices of Black and Hispanic poor people, stating that they should have fewer children, a wholly racist and classist idea."[60] Bennetech and her allies believe that any suggestion that individuals make rational and responsible choices is racial and economic discrimination. However, it is rational and responsible choices that enable one to obtain affordable housing. Irrational and irresponsible choices make it more difficult to afford housing, as demonstrated by Doreen and Larraine.

Some want to reward low-skilled workers regardless of their choices and what they have done to earn a higher wage. Bernie Sanders, for example, has introduced legislation that would increase the federal minimum wage to $15 an hour. The Congressional Budget Office found that this would lift 900,000 people out of poverty. If we look at the issue in isolation, this would seem like a good thing. However, a federal rate of $15 would also result in 1.4 million jobs being lost. The 1.4 million people who lose their job will be the lowest skilled—the very people that the minimum wage is supposed to benefit.

Of course, increasing the minimum wage to $15 will benefit some workers—those fortunate to retain their job. But many will go from a low wage to no wage. Some will make more money, but others will make nothing at all. As we have seen repeatedly, some will benefit at the expense of others. The defenders of raising the minimum wage look at the short-term benefits while evading the long-term consequences. They look at those who will benefit and ignore those who will be harmed by their policies.

This is what happens when the group serves as the standard when evaluating policies. In this instance, Sanders and his ilk look only at the group that will benefit. Even then, they only look at the beneficiaries and ignore the victims. They advocate policies that will benefit one group, while evading what that policy will do to individuals.

Unfortunately, minimum wage laws are not the only limitations on an individual's freedom to earn a living. Occupational licensing does the same thing.

Occupational Licensing Harms The Ambitious

The stated purpose of occupational licensing is to protect consumers from incompetent and unscrupulous practitioners. But licensing is never demanded by consumers. Licensing is always implemented at the request of those already practicing a profession. It is used to create barriers to enter a profession and limit competition. Consider the licensing of florists as an example.

For more than seventy years, florists in Louisiana have been required to obtain a state license before they could legally arrange flowers. An applicant had to pass a written test and a practical examination. The practical examination required an applicant to make four separate arrangements in four hours. The arrangements were then graded by a panel of judges made up of licensed florists. As the Institute for Justice noted at the time:

> To obtain a license, individuals must pass both a written examination and a practical test requiring them to create four themed floral arrangements that are judged by their future competition—florists who already passed the licensing exam. By giving licensed florists the power to decide who is and who is not qualified to arrange flowers, Louisiana gives existing businesses the power to restrict competition.[61]

When the institute filed a lawsuit in 2010 to have Louisiana's licensure laws declared unconstitutional, florists fought back, declaring that licensure was necessary to protect the public by upholding high professional standards.

Those standards, however, simply protect the group—licensed florists. Florists with new ideas in flower arrangement will be rejected by the licensing board, and consumers will never have the opportunity to choose something new and different.

What one individual finds pleasing may be an eyesore to another. What the licensing board considers a proper arrangement may not be what consumers want. But the defenders of licensing didn't want to allow either florists or consumers to find out. The defenders believe that they know what others value and desire. And this is true in every licensed profession. Licensing often prevents innovators from entering a profession and offering new services and products.

In many professions, the process to become licensed requires years of schooling/training and can cost thousands of dollars. For many, these obstacles are nearly insurmountable. And so, because they can't jump through the government's hoops, they are prohibited from starting a business or entering a profession. Consider plumbing as an example.

In the state of Texas, to get a plumber's license, one must have at least 8,000 hours of on-the-job experience—that is four years working full-time. Aspiring plumbers must also take classes on residential, commercial, and industrial plumbing systems, and then pass a test. There is no rational reason why someone who wants to offer basic plumbing services to homeowners should be required to know about industrial plumbing. Again, a personal story illustrates this point.

As a homeowner and the owner of multiple rental properties, I have replaced dozens of faucets and repaired nearly as many toilet toilets. These are simple repairs to make, and I taught myself to do them. I don't have a single hour of apprenticeship, let alone 8,000 hours.

When I can't do a toilet repair, my plumber charges $200 or more to do so. For most repairs, I can buy the parts for about $10 and do the replacement in about 20 minutes. If I decided to offer a toilet repair service, I could charge $100 for the repair. I would make a reasonable profit, and the homeowner would save 50 percent or more. But if I did so, I would be deemed a criminal by the state of Texas.

If an ambitious person wants to start a plumbing business offering very basic and limited services, he is prohibited from doing so legally. He is prohibited from earning a living, not because he is incompetent or unscrupulous, but simply because he hasn't obtained the state's permission to do so. He can't earn more money and make his life better. And this is true in every profession that requires a license. Requirements that hair braiders obtain a cosmetology license are another example.

Jestina Clayton is a native of Sierra Leone in Africa. She had learned the art of hair braiding while growing up. After moving to the United States and graduating college, she was dissatisfied with her pay in an entry-level job. She decided to open a hair braiding business and began advertising on a local website. She was soon threatened with criminal prosecution if she did not remove her ad and obtain a cosmetology license. Clayton could not afford the two years of training and $16,000 required to get a cosmetology license in Utah, and she closed her business.

Clayton wanted to offer a value to willing buyers, but the state of Utah prohibited her from doing so. They prevented her from improving her financial situation by exercising the right to work.

Occupational licensing isn't the only unjust legal barrier to earning a living. Laws that require employers to negotiate with labor unions have the same effect.

Pro-Union Laws

In 1935, the National Labor Relations Act of 1935 (NLRA)

(also known as the Wagner Act) was signed into law. The goal of the Act was to correct the "unequal bargaining power" between an employer and his employees. This was accomplished by compelling the employer to negotiate with a labor union, regardless of the employer's judgment or desires. This legislation gave unions significant power, and union membership grew from about three million when NLRA was signed to more than eight million by the end of the decade.

The Act made it illegal for an employer to interfere or discourage the formation of a labor union by employees or "to refuse to bargain collectively with the representatives of his employees...." The focus of the NLRA was explicitly on the alleged well-being of the group—the union. The individual employee has no voice in the terms and conditions of his employment. Even if he often gets an opportunity to vote on a proposed contract or union leaders, he must go along with the majority. He must subordinate his values and judgment to the group.

Interestingly, the Act sanctioned a policy of legally empowering unions that refused to admit blacks. Richard Rothstein writes, "For the next thirty years, the government protected the bargaining rights of unions that denied African American the privileges of membership or that segregated them into janitorial or other low-paying jobs."[62] As both the Federal Housing Administration and the Veterans Administration did with mortgages, the government was giving one group—white labor unions—political favors while it was simultaneously denying those favors to blacks.

The racist elements of labor laws have long been eliminated. However, businesses are still compelled to negotiate with union representatives. And individual are still required to subordinate their own desires and interests regarding employment terms and conditions to the desires and interests of the group.

For example, an individual may not want or need all of the perks and benefits the union gains through collective bargaining. A young, healthy, single individual may decide that he does not need health insurance for the time being. Or, he might be willing to work for a lower wage than that demanded by the union. He loses these options when he is required to allow the union to represent him.

Morally, pro-union laws shackle those who are more productive and ambitious. The union, not the employer, often determines the pay and position of its members. Salary increases and promotions are often determined by seniority, not productivity and merit. With the focus on the group, more deserving individuals are subordinate to the less deserving.

To be clear. I am not anti-union. I am opposed to the government forcing employers to negotiate with unions. Government should be protecting the freedom of individuals to engage in voluntary agreements. That includes the freedom to join a union or not, as well as the freedom to negotiate with a union or not.

The Freedom To Choose

The three policy areas that we have examined in this chapter prevent individuals from acting on their choices. Minimum wage, occupational licensing, and pro-union laws prevent individuals from acting as they think best for their own lives. Preventing individuals from acting as they deem best is disempowering. That is the inevitable result of the Progressive framework and setting the collective as the standard of value.

When an individual is disempowered, he loses control over his own life. He is dependent on the decisions and choices of others. He is subordinate to the group.

If we want to enable individuals to live flourishing lives, then we must protect their freedom to choose, as well as the freedom to act on their choices. This means rejecting the group as the standard in every aspect of life and in every policy issue.

Policies that prevent us from acting on our own judgment imply that we can't make rational decisions. We must allow government officials to make choices for us. And while those officials claim that they will lead us to the promised land, they have actually led us to our current housing crisis.

Ostensibly, minimum wage laws and pro-union laws are intended to empower individuals and provide more opportunities. But these laws do not empower the individuals who are no longer free to choose the terms of their employment.

THE FRAMEWORK OF THE PAST

Each of the housing related policies that we have examined used one group or another as the standard by which to evaluate that policy. These policies have been evaluated through the lens of the benefits to the favored group.

Zoning was initially used to benefit one group—whites—and then it was expanded to benefit another group—"the community." Through the Department of Housing and Urban Development, government has sought to benefit one group—low-income households—with subsidized housing. The Federal Housing Administration, along with the Veterans Administration, Freddie Mac, and Fannie Mae, has provided subsidies for one group—first white home buyers and then low-income households. Monetary policy has been used to benefit the group—"the public." Tax policy is used to benefit one group—homeowners. Regulatory policies have been used to benefit two groups—low-income households and minorities. Road policy was initially used to benefit one group—motorists—and then became a massive benefit to another group—suburbanites. Minimum wage laws are used to benefit one group—low-skilled workers. Occupational licensing is intended to benefit another group—"the public." Pro-union laws are used to provide benefits to one group—labor union members.

From the perspective of the favored group, these policies have generally been effective. Single-family zoning has allowed many neighborhoods to keep multi-family housing beyond its borders. Subsidies for homeowners have increased home ownership. Pro-union laws have forced employers to negotiate with union representatives. But while these policies are benefitting one group, they are inflicting harm on others. Single-family zoning often prevents low-income households from living in more desirable neighborhoods. Road policy has required the seizure and demolition of affordable housing. Occupational licensing prevents ambitious individuals from entering a profession or starting a business. Unfortunately, those who will be harmed are seldom considered. The benefits to the favored group are all that matters.

In focusing on the group, each of these policies is considered in isolation—how it will affect the favored group. The injustice to others is ignored. For example, single-family zoning benefits those who share the "community's values," but it is unjust to property owners who desire a different use for their land. Minimum wage laws are unjust to low-skilled workers who want the opportunity to gain work experience and are willing to work for a lower pay. Housing subsidies are unjust to the taxpayers who are forced to foot the housing bill for others.

To those who embrace the Progressive framework, the long-term consequences of a policy are impossible to predict, and thus, cannot be considered. For example, providing motorists with subsidized roads drives up the demand, has led to congested roads, and demands for more highways. Single-family zoning drives up the cost of land, and thus, the cost of housing. Forcing lenders to extend risky mortgage to individuals with poor credit results in financial catastrophe. All of these could have been foreseen if the full context had been considered.

Each of these policies has contributed to the unaffordability of housing to one degree or another. In combination, they have made it increasingly difficult for individuals to attain the housing that want. These policies have contributed to reduced justice in regard to housing.

The housing crisis is the result of the Progressive

framework, of compelling individuals to do the "right" thing. That framework regards the government hammer as the only available tool, and every problem, including those created by that hammer, is a nail. Unfortunately, though the housing crisis has grown worse over the decades, that framework has not been abandoned.

PART 3

The Present

*We cannot solve our problems with the same thinking
we used when we created them.* Albert Einstein

In Part 2, we saw how a variety of government policies have impacted the affordability of housing. For more than a century, governments at all levels have interfered with the freedom of housing producers and the ability of individuals to improve their financial circumstances. The policies enacted by government were the consequence of the flawed Progressive framework.

The pandemic and resulting economic turmoil have made the situation worse, and government officials have been attempting to address the affordable housing problem. Unfortunately, they are following the same framework that created the problem.

It is said that those who do not learn from history are doomed to repeat it. Government officials have not learned the proper lessons from past failures. Rather than reject the flawed framework that led to those failures, they have embraced that framework and attempted to apply it differently. But the same framework will lead to the same results, no matter what tweaking legislators and bureaucrats do. In Part 3 we will examine contemporary policies and proposals, as well as the framework underlying them.

Many of the policies that we will examine have been enacted into law. Others are still being debated by legislators and may or may not be enacted. The cogent point here is the framework being used to discuss the affordable housing crisis and potential solutions.

UPZONING

As we saw in Chapter 4, one of the primary causes for the housing crisis is single-family zoning (SFZ), also called exclusionary zoning. In prohibiting denser housing construction, SFZ effectively removes land from development. A lot that could hold housing for multiple families is limited to housing for one family. This drives up the cost of land, and with it, the cost of housing.

SFZ prohibits duplexes, triplexes, accessory dwelling units (also called "granny flats" or "mother-in-law suites,") as well as small apartment buildings and condominiums. Much of the land in the nation's residential neighborhoods consists of lawns, patios, and decks. While many Americans prefer these amenities, SFZ arbitrarily prohibits others from creating more housing on their property.

As the term implies, the purpose of exclusionary zoning is to exclude, to keep certain types of people out of a neighborhood. Initially, zoning laws were explicitly racist and excluded minorities. When those were declared unconstitutional, cities turned to single-family zoning to accomplish essentially the same purpose. In terms of housing costs, multi-family housing is generally less expensive than single-family housing. In prohibiting multi-family housing, SFZ makes housing in designated neighborhoods unaffordable for low-income families. The result is economic and racial segregation.

Recognizing the destructive nature of SFZ, a growing number of cities and states have enacted or considered measures to eliminate or relax exclusionary zoning laws. This is often called upzoning. Relaxing zoning laws may seem to be a rejection of the framework of the past. However, those who advocate allowing denser housing development base their argument on the same Progressive framework that led to SFZ.

Relaxing Single-Family Zoning Laws

In 2018, Minneapolis became the first city to abolish SFZ. The city council adopted an ordinance that allowed duplexes and triplexes on nearly every lot in the city previously designated for single-family homes. In 2019, Oregon passed a law that requires cities with a population greater than 10,000 to permit duplexes in neighborhoods previously limited to single-family homes. In 2021, Berkeley, California, the birthplace of single-family zoning repealed that designation for all land within the city, and Charlotte's city council voted to allow duplexes and triplexes throughout much of the city. The North Carolina legislature considered a bill in 2021 that would eliminate SFZ in the state, but the bill died in committee.

California, which is home to some of the nation's most draconian land-use regulations, has been a surprising leader in relaxing single-family zoning. In 2019, the state legislature legalized accessory dwelling units (ADUs) in areas previously limited to single-family homes. The results were immediate and dramatic. Permits for ADUs increased from 728 in 2014 to 14,702 in 2019.[63]

Then, in 2021 the legislature passed two bills that pave the way for cities throughout the state to end SFZ. Senate Bill 9 allows property owners to subdivide their lot, thereby permitting additional housing to be built. Senate Bill 10, according to a press release from California Gov. Gavin Newsome,

> creates a voluntary process for local governments to access a streamlined zoning process for new multi-unit housing near transit or in urban infill areas, with up to 10 units per parcel. The legislation simplifies the CEQA [California Environmental

Quality Act] requirements for upzoning, giving local leaders another tool to voluntarily increase density.[64]

While Senate Bill 10 is a step in the right direction, many cities are refusing to allow denser development. Those cities want to retain exclusionary zoning.

A key aspect of California's efforts is reducing the regulatory burden on property owners. A streamlined permitting process eliminates many of the delays and expenses that drive up the cost of housing. CEQA is a particularly onerous land-use regulation. It requires local and state governments to consider the potential environmental effects of a project before deciding whether to approve it. It also allows private parties to file lawsuits to stop or amend projects based on the potential environmental impact of a project. CEQA has been used to stop or dramatically alter countless development projects.

As one example, several environmental groups filed a lawsuit in 2012 against a developer who wanted to build sixty-five homes on a one hundred thirteen-acre site. After the developer received unanimous approval from the Orange County Board of Supervisors, a number of environmental groups sued under the provisions of CEQA. In a previous attempt to appease the environmental groups, the developer had donated 1,140 acres to conservation groups. In other words, the developer simply gave away 90 percent of his land, and environmentalists were still not satisfied. One of the groups opposed to the development wrote that, "the county has managed to degrade the planning process by turning it into a kind of source for private gain rather than an instrument of the public good that it is supposed to be."[65] Even though the developer "voluntarily" sacrificed 90 percent of his property for the "public good," environmentalists wanted him to sacrifice even more. Even though he had subordinated himself to the group, environmentalists wanted the group to exert further control over him.

Ideally, such anti-development laws should be repealed

rather than just relaxed. A destructive policy remains destructive even when relaxed, though not as egregiously. In the meantime, relaxing the requirements under CEQA and similar laws is a positive step. Unfortunately, relaxing the regulatory burden on housing producers isn't supported by everyone.

The Debate Over Single-Family Zoning

As a part of his housing plan, President Biden has proposed that states and municipalities receiving certain federal grants be required to eliminate SFZ. Biden has said that exclusionary zoning perpetuates policies that have been used to "keep people of color and low-income families out of certain neighborhoods." While it is true that exclusionary zoning has been used for racial and economic segregation, Biden's focus is on groups—people of color and low-income families—rather than individuals. And a focus on groups rather than individuals perpetuates the same Progressive framework that led to exclusionary zoning in the first place.

Some supporters of Biden's plan are concerned that it contains "too many carrots and few sticks."[66] In other words, while the plan would give incentives to states and municipalities to eliminate SFZ, there isn't a mandate to do so. This is essentially what is happening in California. The fact that the law allows municipalities to do something doesn't mean that they will do it.

A rights-respecting federal government would abolish SFZ across the nation. Land-use regulations are unjust—they penalize property owners simply because they are property owners. Rather than provide incentives to jurisdictions to eliminate SFZ, Biden should propose legislation to completely eliminate SFZ across the nation. The states and local governments are not exempt from abiding by the Constitution and protecting individual rights, including property rights. The federal government can and should intervene when jurisdictions violate individual rights with laws like SFZ. But to pursue that policy would require a new framework, a framework founded on individualism rather than collectivism.

Unfortunately, the current efforts to eliminate or relax SFZ are a matter of political expediency rather than principle. Evaluating SFZ in isolation, the advocates of these policies see a problem and seek to solve it without consideration of the broader issues and principles involved. For example, they fail to consider the fact that, if SFZ is detrimental to the production of affordable housing, then other land-use regulations must also play a role. To its credit, the California legislature seems to have grasped this fact, at least partially, when it relaxed the CEQA process. However, that too was a matter of expediency rather than a matter of principle. If it were a matter of principle, legislators would call for an end to every law that impedes the production of housing, rather than just those that are politically unpopular.

By embracing the same framework as the advocates of SFZ, opponents of exclusionary zoning undermine their own arguments. They are trying to reverse the effects of a flawed framework while clinging to that framework. By focusing on groups rather than individuals, they are missing a powerful piece of intellectual ammunition. By focusing on groups, they cannot frame the issue in terms of the injustice that SFZ imposes upon individuals. And that explains much of the push back against proposals to eliminate SFZ.

The focus on groups dominates discussions of housing policy, even among critics of Biden's plan. Conservative Betsy McCaughey, former Lieutenant Governor of New York and one-time economic advisor to Donald Trump, writes that eliminating single-family zoning would be disastrous for America's suburbs:

> Biden's plan is to force suburban towns with single-family homes and minimum lot sizes to build high-density affordable housing smack in the middle of their leafy neighborhood—local preferences and local control be damned. [67]

To McCaughey and other conservatives, the preferences of the group should supersede the preferences of individual property owners. Zoning is good, they argue, because it is a tool used to impose the values of the group—the community—upon all property owners

Another critic of Biden's plan is Progressive David Imbroscio. He writes,

> While it is clear that EZ [exclusionary zoning] measures often (though not always) both reflect and perpetuate the ubiquitous racism and white supremacy that profoundly corrupt the promise of America, the project to eliminate them inflicts a greater degree of racialized suffering upon those disadvantaged by both class standing and skin color. In short, the Anti-EZ cure is worse—much worse, in fact—than the EZ disease.[68]

Like Biden and McCaughey, Imbroscio's standard is the alleged welfare of the group. Like Biden, Imbroscio thinks that the preferred group should be low-income people of color. But regardless of the particular group that they focus on, each embraces the Progressive framework that the group is supreme. Not surprisingly, they all advocate policies that differ in detail but align in principle. All agree that the group is the standard of value. Each proposes to use the coercive power of government to subordinate individuals to the group that he thinks is most important and in a way that he believes will be most effective.

Biden, McCaughey, and Imbroscio are looking at exclusionary zoning from the limited perspective of alleged benefits to his preferred group. Biden considers SFZ harmful because it it is harmful to low-income families and people of color. McCaughey considers SFZ good because it allows a neighborhood to promote and protect the values of the community. And Imbroscio thinks eliminating SFZ will cause more harm than good to minorities and low-income families. When a policy debate focuses on groups, the only issue that must be decided is which group will prevail. When one examines an issue from a limited perspective, one is incapable of examining the full context. And this is not the only evasion occurring in the debate over SFZ.

Single-Family Zoning And Property Rights

Some have argued that eliminating SFZ would be a violation of property rights because denser development diminishes property values. However, the right to property means the freedom to produce, use, and trade material values. Morally, there is no such thing as a right to endlessly appreciating property values. Practically, at least two studies have found that denser development actually increases the value of nearby single-family homes.

In early 2021, the Kem C. Gardner Policy Institute at the University of Utah, released a study that examined the impact of high-density apartments on single-family home values in suburban Salt Lake County. The study found,

> Between 2010 and 2019, homes located within ½ mile of a newly constructed apartment building experienced a 10.0% average annual increase in median value, while the value of those farther away increased by 8.6%.[69]

Similarly, an analysis of the impact of eliminating SFZ in Minneapolis compared home sales prices for single-family homes three kilometers inside of the city border to sales prices for homes three kilometers outside of the city border. (Areas outside of the city had retained SFZ.) The study found that homes within the city increased by 3 to 5 percent more than those outside the city. The study's author notes "that this increase is to be expected, since greater development potential raises the immediate value of previously single-family properties, even though in the long-term it can encourage a broader housing supply, which can lower city-wide housing prices."[70] While other factors may play a role in the differences found in both Salt Lake and Minneapolis, eliminating SFZ does not reduce property values.

Other opponents to SFZ argue that many people bought their home expecting to live in a single-family neighborhood. To change zoning designations after the fact would violate their property rights. Again, the right to property means the freedom to produce, use, and trade material values. Zoning violates this freedom by dictating what property owners can and cannot do with their property. To claim that restoring freedom to property owners violates property rights is a perversion of the concept.

When zoning laws were explicitly racist, many bought homes expecting to live in a whites-only neighborhood. Such laws were an injustice because they prohibited individuals from producing, using, and trading property as they deemed best. No rational person would claim that eliminating racist zoning laws is a violation of property rights. Yet, in principle, that is the position of those claiming that eliminating SFZ would violate the right to property.

The entire discussion of SFZ is framed using the same premises that originally gave rise to exclusionary zoning. Those on both sides of the issue view some group—whether low-income families, minorities, suburbanites, or homeowners—as the standard of value. Both sides argue that it is proper for government to use coercion to impose the values of the group upon every individual in the community. Both sides agree that individuals should be subservient to the collective.

While many are welcoming the end of exclusionary zoning, some see it as an opportunity to implement a policy called inclusionary zoning. A growing number of cities are requiring developers to include below-market rate housing in their projects in exchange for government approval of requests to upzone a parcel of land. The purpose of inclusionary zoning is to avoid displacement of low-income households and minorities when new housing is built. On the one hand, exclusionary zoning is used to keep certain kinds of people out of a neighborhood. On the other hand, inclusionary zoning is used to keep certain kinds of people in a neighborhood.

Inclusionary zoning is simply the other side of the

exclusionary zoning coin. Both forms of zoning impose restrictions and requirements on property owners. Both are founded on the premise that government policy should benefit one group or another. Both are founded on the belief that it is proper for government to use force to achieve desired results.

Eliminating SFZ and allowing for greater housing density is a crucial part of addressing the housing shortage. But those who want to end exclusionary zoning cannot embrace the same framework as exclusionary zoning's defenders.

Reasonable Expectations

Eliminating SFZ will not have an immediate, large-scale impact anywhere in the country. The affordable housing crisis was not created overnight, and it won't be resolved overnight. But with their freedom partially restored, property owners can begin to consider new and better uses for their land. Houston, which has never had comprehensive zoning in any form, provides an example of what can happen when property owners can change land uses without groveling at the feet of government bureaucrats.

In one area near downtown—Mid Town—row houses and dilapidated public housingwere replaced with apartments, condominiums, single-family homes, and townhomes. The redevelopment attracted restaurants, bars, and retail businesses. Over the course of about fifteen years, the previously impoverished neighborhood was transformed into a vibrant, walkable community. The same thing has occurred in many of Houston's neighborhoods because property owners have the freedom to use their property in the manner that they deem best.

Many complain that this type of redevelopment displaces long-time residents as housing prices and property taxes rise. This is undeniably true, and the issue of gentrification will be dealt with more thoroughly in Chapter 14. For now, suffice it to say that freedom in land use is just because it protects the rights of property owners to use their land as they deem best.

In discussing the issue of single-family zoning, we must reject the Progressive framework that the group as the standard of value. That framework leaves us debating which group should receive benefits and which individuals should provide those benefits. No matter which group is favored, the individual is caught in the crossfire.

Instead, we must embrace a framework that holds individual liberty as the standard. We must examine policies from the perspective of what is good for individuals—all individuals—not groups.

TENANT PROTECTIONS

For years, the "tenants' rights"[71] movement has been growing in both supporters and influence. The economic problems caused by the pandemic have strengthened the movement and led to political victories across the country.

Activist Jen Deerinwater, in a piece titled "What Does Housing Justice Really Mean?" writes that, "I want a future where housing is free for Black, Indigenous, and other people of color (BIPOC), for people with disabilities, for people who don't make much money."[72] In March 2020, Rep. Pramilla Jayapal introduced the Housing is a Human Right Act of 2020. An editorial in the Los Angeles Times in 2021 declared that the solution to homelessness in California is declaring a right to housing. "A right to housing has a simple but powerful underpinning," the editorial states, "The government should ensure that everyone has an adequate home."[73] The Housing Justice National Platform argues that "[h]ousing and land should be democratically owned and controlled by community members...."[74]

Housing, the movement asserts, should not be bought and sold like a commodity. Whether implicitly or explicitly, housing activists want government to shield renters from market forces.

The essence of the movement is the belief that housing is a fundamental human right. This belief had been gaining in popularity before the pandemic, but the threat of mass evictions and foreclosures, along with sympathetic legislators, has given housing activists additional vigor and broadened support for recognizing housing as a right. Tenant protections are the most common means for implementing this policy.

To this end, the movement has successfully convinced legislators across the country to enact laws to protect tenants in a variety of ways. While the details of these laws vary, the underlying premise is that rights apply to groups, not individuals. Each attempts to address a perceived problem in isolation. These laws are founded on the Progressive framework.

Rights: What They Are And Aren't

Rights pertain to freedom of action. Rights protect the freedom of an individual to act as he judges best in the pursuit of the values he desires, so long as he respects the freedom of others to act as they judge best in the pursuit of the values that they desire.

There is no such thing as "tenants' rights." Such a claim implies that tenants have rights that are separate and distinct from non-renters. It implies that tenants should be free to take certain actions, but that property owners should be prohibited from taking the same or similar actions.

When rights are applied to groups, a conflict of "rights" is in the inevitable result. The rights of one group are seen to conflict with the rights of non-members of that group. As an example, according to this framework, the rights of tenants conflict with the rights of landlords. And, according to this framework, the only way to protect the alleged rights of one group is by violating the rights of individuals who are not a member of the favored group.

However, rights do not apply to groups. They apply to individuals—all individuals. Each individual, renter or landlord, developer or homebuyer, rich or poor, black or white, has the same right to freely act as he thinks best. When rights are applied to individuals, they do not conflict. Rights protect our freedom to interact with others voluntarily, with each agreeing to the terms and conditions of that interaction. When an agreement can't be reached, each is free to go his own way.

Our rights place boundaries on what others can do. In short, they can't prevent us from acting as we choose. The only way to prevent us from acting on our choices is through physical force or the threat thereof. Only by tying us up, waving a gun in our face, or threatening us harm can another individual stop us from acting as we judge best. Fundamentally, rights means the abolition of force from human relations.

But the tenant protections movement is not seeking freedom of action for renters. The movement is seeking to deny landlords and developers freedom of action. The movement wants government to impose controls and restrictions on landlords and developers. They want to use physical force or the threat of force, such as fines or jail, to prevent housing providers from acting on their judgment. This is an injustice to landlords and a violation of their actual rights. There is no such thing as a right to violate the rights of others.

Further, the "right to housing" implies that individuals should be provided housing regardless of, or despite, their own actions. The movement implicitly argues that the mere fact that an individual exists gives him a claim to the values that life requires.

Again, rights pertain to freedom of action. Each individual has a right to take the actions he believes will enable him to attain the values he desires, including housing. Values, including housing, do not exist free for the taking. Values, including housing, must be produced. Rights protect our freedom to produce the housing we desire, or produce comparable values that we can trade with others to acquire the housing we desire.

If housing is a right, then landlords, builders, developers, and taxpayers have a moral obligation to provide housing for others. And they must do so regardless of their own judgment or desires. This means that housing producers must produce for the benefit of others, regardless of their own desires or judgment. This is nothing more than slavery, and there is no justice in slavery.

If housing is a right, then those who do not provide housing for renters are guilty of violating the rights of tenants. This is the type of conflict that inevitably arises when one asserts a right to a value. Some must be forced to produce so that others can consume. Just as rights do not apply to groups, there is no such thing as the right to a value. The false claims that groups possess rights and housing is a right are founded on the Progressive framework.

The tenant protections movement wants to use the coercive power of government to force builders, landlords, and developers to provide a value—housing—for low-income families on terms dictated by government. The movement claims that such actions are necessary to balance the power between landlords and tenants. This equates economic power with political power.

Economic power is the power to produce. Political power is the power to coerce. Economic power is gained by producing values that others desire and willingly pay for. Political power is gained by influencing legislators to pass laws restricting and controlling the actions of others. Housing activists seek to use political power to control economic power. They seek to use coercion to force property owners to act as the activists think proper.

When one cannot convince another individual to voluntarily act as he desires, one has two choices: 1. Accept the right of others to choose for themselves, or. 2. Force them to act in the desired manner. The robber uses the threat of force to obtain values that the rightful owner would not voluntarily give him. A rapist uses force to obtain non-consensual sex.

Force negates thought and choices. Force is used to compel individuals to act in a manner that they wouldn't voluntarily choose. Indeed, the purpose of force is to compel individuals to act contrary to their judgment. This is precisely what housing activists seek.

To be fair, housing producers have not been completely

innocent in this regard. National trade organizations, such as National Association of Realtors and the National Association of Home Builders, regularly lobby for legislation that provides benefits for their members. Awarding special political favors to housing producers is just as wrong as awarding special political favors to housing consumers. Government officials should not be awarding special political favors to anyone.

There are a number of ways that legislators award special favors to renters under the guise of tenant protections. We will examine some of the most popular.

Eviction Moratoriums

Perhaps the most obvious tenant protection is the eviction moratoriums invoked during the pandemic. In September 2020, the Centers for Disease Control and Prevention (CDC) issued a national moratorium on evictions for non-payment of rent. Originally slated to end on December 31, 2020 the moratorium was extended several more times before the United States Supreme Court ruled in October 2021 that the moratorium exceeded the CDC's authority.

The stated purpose of the moratoriums was to prevent individuals suffering financial hardship because of the pandemic from losing their home. Landlords were forced to continue providing a value without compensation, regardless of their own desires or needs and without any legal recourse. At the same time, landlords had to continue paying the mortgage, insurance, property taxes, and maintenance costs despite receiving diminished or no income. Though the moratoriums did not absolve renters from paying the accumulated rental debt, it should have been immediately clear that someone who was months behind on the rent was unlikely to suddenly come up with the money. Eviction moratoriums are an attempt to help renters by imposing an injustice on landlords.

The eviction moratoriums illustrate the consequences of the Progressive framework. At the beginning of the pandemic, businesses were forced to shut down to deal with the immediate problem of "flattening the curve." The long-term consequences were evaded until it was too late. Public officials refused to consider the full context. Tens of millions lost their jobs and many could not pay their rent. The moratoriums were enacted in an attempt to address a problem created by earlier government policies.

In the absence of an eviction moratorium, most landlords would try to work with tenants facing financial problems. An eviction can be an expensive and time-consuming process, and most property owners prefer to avoid evictions when possible. As an example, several months into the pandemic, a long-time tenant lost her job and she was unable to pay the full rent. I offered her a 30 percent discount for a four-month period. I preferred to keep her as a tenant rather that pursue an eviction. If I had evicted her, I would have had to pay more than $300 in court costs. Once I gained possession of the property, I would have had to paint, clean, and make repairs. The average cost for this is over $2,000. I would also have been deprived of income while the eviction was processing, during the make-ready, and then while I found another tenant. The total cost for an eviction can easily be over $5,000. Offering the discount was beneficial to both of us.

In response to the cascading economic destruction caused by the lock downs, legislators responded with a number of programs to aid tenants. While rental assistance did help many families pay past due rent and remain in their home, many did not apply for aid or were not accepted into one of the programs. When the moratoriums began expiring, a looming tsunami of evictions concerned both housing activists and legislators. Many responded by demanding another tenant protection—the right to counsel.

The Right To Counsel

Housing advocates argue that when tenants are facing eviction, they have an unfair disadvantage. They claim that landlords are represented by an attorney nearly 90 percent of the time, while tenants have legal representation only 10 percent of the time. I find this claim dubious given my own personal experiences.

I have been to eviction court more than ten times. Each time, there were dozens of other cases on the docket. I have been present for well over one-hundred eviction cases, and I have seen an attorney present for a landlord only one time. And that was an apartment complex that was evicting multiple tenants that day. All of my evictions have been for non-payment of rent, and only three tenants even bothered to show up for the trial. Each tenant who did attend admitted to the judge that she hadn't paid the rent. These were simple cases, and there was no dispute over the facts. There was no need for an attorney to be involved.

Regardless of the actual statistics, housing advocates demand that tenants be provided free legal help when facing an eviction, just as defendants in a criminal case are provided a public defender. At least nine cities have enacted "right to counsel" laws, including Seattle, Louisville, and Cleveland.

When tenants are provided a taxpayer funded attorney, landlords are going to have little choice but to hire one themselves. I certainly did. After losing an eviction hearing, the tenant appealed and filed a pauper's affidavit. She was provided a pro bono attorney for the appeal. Despite handling all of my previous evictions without an attorney, I thought it prudent to hire one for the appeal. It should be obvious, but hiring an attorney costs money. And when a landlord's expenses increase, rents are soon to follow. Providing legal counsel for tenants facing eviction will certainly help some, but other renters will face higher rents. Adding insult to injury, the landlord will also have the privilege of helping pay for the tenant's attorney through his taxes. Right to counsel laws subordinate landlords and taxpayers to renters.

Along with other tenant protections, the right to counsel is going to discourage property owners from renting housing. And those who stay in the business are going to be much more discerning when screening tenants. However, housing advocates are already working to make screening much more difficult for landlords through "ban the box" laws.

Ban The Box

According to Wikipedia, "ban the box" originally began as a

> campaign by advocates for ex-offenders, aimed at removing the check box that asks if applicants have a criminal record from hiring applications. Its purpose is to enable ex-offenders to display their qualifications in the hiring process before being asked about their criminal records. The premise of the campaign is that anything that makes it harder for ex-offenders to find a job makes it likelier that they will re-offend, which is bad for society.[75]

The premise is that the group—society—is the standard of value. The campaign has been successful. Since 1998, 37 states and over 150 cities and counties have adopted ban the box laws. Advocates for convicted criminals are now turning their efforts to housing applications, seeking to eliminate what they consider a discriminatory practice. At least three cities have passed such laws.

In December 2020, Montgomery County, Maryland became one of the first jurisdictions to enact a ban the box law for housing. The law prohibits landlords from conducting a criminal background check prior to offering a property to a tenant. And after making that offer, the landlord is prohibited from asking about convictions for such offenses as trespassing, misdemeanor theft, and indecent exposure. A sponsor of the bill said, "Nobody should be denied housing because they couldn't afford to pay a traffic ticket while they were experiencing homelessness."[76] Equating trespassing, misdemeanor theft, and indecent exposure to the failure to pay a traffic ticket is disingenuous. These are fundamentally different actions.

In June 2021, New Jersey became the first state to pass a ban the box law for housing. Like Montgomery County, the law prohibits landlords from asking about criminal convictions prior to making an offer to the tenant. After conducting a background check,

> The law encourages landlords who find criminal offenses to weigh the nature of the crime, the length of time passed, and how the offense would affect the safety of the landlord's property and other tenants. If the landlord decides to withdraw their offer, they must explain their reversal.[77]

The landlord, not the person with a criminal record, is the one who must explain himself. And if the tribunal reviewing his reason for withdrawing an offer finds it unacceptable, the landlord could be forced to rent his property against his own judgment.

Ban the box advocates argue that considering an applicant's criminal record is a form of discrimination and should be illegal. They are correct that it is a form of discrimination; they are wrong to argue that it should be illegal.

To discriminate means to identify differences between two or more things. Every choice we make is an act of discrimination. We discriminate when we decide what movie to watch, what restaurant to dine at, which sports teams we support, which people we befriend. There is a difference between horror films and romantic comedies, between fast food and an upscale restaurant, between the Cowboys and the Jets, between a thief and an honest individual. The choices that we make are based on our personal values.

In regard to housing, we must consider the full context. A landlord proposes to rent his property to a stranger. He wants some assurance that the individual will be responsible and respect the property. He wants some understanding of the tenant's character, and past actions, while not a perfect indicator, certainly provide valuable information. Past actions are a part of an individual's context.

An individual with a long criminal record possesses a much different character than an individual with a clean record.

Yet, ban the box advocates want landlords to treat the two equally. They want the convicted criminal to be treated the same as the law-abiding citizen. Indeed, an opinion piece published by several websites states, "Savannahians with criminal records deserve same opportunities afforded other citizens."[78] There is no justice in forcing landlords to ignore certain facts. Justice demands that we treat others as they have earned by their words and actions. Ban the box makes this impossible. In fact, such laws make landlords criminals for attempting to make rational choices. Ban the box subordinates individuals to the group.

And it's not enough to prohibit landlords from considering a tenant's criminal history, a growing number of advocates are demanding that landlords be prohibited from considering past evictions. Again, context matters. An individual who has been evicted has demonstrated a much different character than a tenant who has never been evicted. But housing advocates don't want landlords to consider character. They want everyone treated the same, regardless of their past actions, or in spite of them.

Many landlords, myself included, do not automatically reject an applicant with a criminal history or a past eviction. When I discover such things, I consider when the offense occurred and the nature of the crime. A conviction for possession of marijuana fifteen years ago is not a concern. A conviction for armed robbery is, no matter when the latter was committed. Similarly, I do not consider a tenant with an eviction fifteen years ago and a clean record since to pose a significant risk. But what is acceptable is a decision that each landlord should be free to make.

While ban the box laws limit the property owner's ability to screen a tenant, they do nothing to eliminate his legal liabilities should a tenant prove to be a danger to other individuals. The landlord will be held responsible even though his ability to make a responsible choice was restricted by the law. Indeed, ban the box laws are about absolving those with criminal convictions or past evictions while holding landlords accountable for the tenant's future actions.

Some housing advocates want further measures to protect tenants from the consequences of their actions. They want to essentially eliminate evictions.

"Just Cause Eviction"

"Just cause eviction" laws (sometimes called "good cause eviction laws) are, according to housing advocate Shelter Force, "a legal framework that requires landlords to provide sufficient grounds for any attempt to remove a tenant from [sic] through eviction...."[79] Currently, four states and more than twenty cities have just cause eviction laws. While the details vary, such laws can literally hold a landlord hostage.

A good cause bill considered in New York State would have given tenants the "right" to renew a lease regardless of the landlord's desire. A New York City Councilmember who supports the state bill acknowledged the problems the law might impose on small landlords. But those problems, he said, are minor compared to that of tenants facing eviction. "The trauma for tenants who get evicted in a tight real estate market is far more severe than the challenges facing a small landlord,"[80] he said. And so, he has no qualms about imposing problems on landlords for the alleged benefit of tenants. He has no qualms about subordinating individuals to the group.

Another supporter of the bill, Ithaca, New York, alderman Ducson Nguyen, wrote "good landlords have nothing to fear from good cause eviction legislation. But the protection such a law provides is essential for preventing housing discrimination."[81] Apparently, a landlord who renews leases indiscriminately is "good," and landlords who don't are bad. And bad landlords should be forced to do to do the "right" thing as defined by housing activists. Individuals should not be free to act as they deem best. They can only act as the collective permits.

Just cause eviction laws create a one-sided relationship. They give the tenant a choice, but they deny choice for the landlord. And the same is true of renters' choice laws

Renters' Choice

Renters' choice give tenants the option of paying a security deposit (often one month's rent) or buying security deposit insurance (SDI). SDI payments are very inexpensive, about $5 a month for a property renting for $1,000. SDI allows tenants with little savings to be able to move into a new home without the burden of a large security deposit. To date, Atlanta, Baltimore, and Cincinnati have passed renter's choice laws.

The Atlanta law also gives tenants the option to pay the security deposit in three payments. Cincinnati gives tenants three options: SDI, pay the security deposit over six months, or a reduced security deposit not to exceed 50 percent of the first month's rent. A renters' choice bill was introduced in the North Carolina legislature in 2021 but was not passed.

The website for Renter Choice imply that such laws are a win-win, that both tenants and landlords benefit.[82] If this is true, then landlords would voluntarily offer the option of SDI and legislators wouldn't have to force them to accept SDI. It is presumptuous for these activists to claim to know what is best for landlords.

A landlord may not like the idea of SDI. I certainly wouldn't accept SDI. Any claims will require an inspection or documentation and impose additional costs and delays. A tenant could dispute a claim and prolong the process. A tenant could cancel the insurance policy and leave the landlord with little recourse. "Renters' choice" laws give renters options while removing the landlord's options. Like right to renew, renters' choice gives tenants the freedom to choose while denying the landlord the freedom to choose.

Assorted Protections

The above tenant protections aren't enough for some housing

activists and their legislative supporters. They are advocating, and passing, an assortment of other laws.

Seattle passed a law requiring landlords to give at least a six-month notice of a rent increase. And if a tenant chooses to move because of a rent increase, the landlord must pay the tenant the equivalent of three month's rent.

Context matters. It can be very difficult for a landlord to know his future expenses six months in advance. Property tax bills are received once a year. Insurance policies renew once a year. If both of these occur within six months of a lease renewal, the landlord has no means to recover the additional costs. And if he raises the rent to be safe and the tenant moves, he is stuck with paying the tenant.

This type of law makes it impossible for property owners to make rational decisions. But as we have seen, housing activists aren't concerned with the landlord's ability to make rational decisions. They want the landlord to act a certain way, and they are willing to use the coercive power of government to make him.

Ann Arbor, Michigan passed a law that prohibits landlords from showing a property until 150 days before a lease expires. As a college town, landlords have a high rate of turnover. They want to get their properties renewed or rented as soon as possible. Whether a landlord needs more than 150 days to renew or rent isn't the issue. The issue is that his choices are limited by what the city council dictates.

These laws illustrate the turmoil being imposed on landlords. On one hand, Seattle is unjustly requiring landlords to plan at least six months in advance. On the other hand, Ann Arbor unjustly prohibits landlords from planning that far in advance.

In September 2021, Ann Arbor became the third jurisdiction in the country to create a "Renters Commission" to make recommendations to the city council. Unlike similar commissions in Seattle and King County, Washington, Ann Arbor will allow landlords to have several seats on the commission. However, the landlords won't be able to vote on any policy recommendations, which makes their inclusion on the commission meaningless.

All of the tenant protections that we have examined impose restrictions and controls on property owners for the alleged benefit of tenants. Despite the claims of housing activists, tenant protection laws are an injustice.

The Injustice Of Tenant Protections

Each of these protections are evaluated in isolation without consideration of the full context. For example, the eviction moratoriums created serious financial difficulties for many landlords. Many are getting out of the rental business, which leaves fewer homes available for renters. While most tenants have tried to pay their rent, many took advantage of the moratorium to receive free housing. Since they couldn't be evicted for non-payment, they didn't pay. The moratoriums have provided a cover for irresponsible behavior and allowed the guilty to go unpunished while the innocent landlord is penalized. There is no justice in granting unearned benefits or dispensing undeserved punishment.

As another example, ban the box laws force landlords to treat convicted criminals and those with past evictions the same as individuals with a clean record. Invariably, some with a clean record will be denied housing in deference to someone with convictions or evictions. There is no justice in making the innocent suffer while the guilty benefit.

As a final example, the right to counsel is going to prolong the eviction process and add to the property owner's expenses. This will eventually result in higher rents as landlords seek to recover their costs. All renters will suffer for the benefit of the few who faced eviction. Indeed, all of these tenant protections benefit some at the expense of others. All make individuals secondary to the alleged well-being of the collective.

Each of the tenant protections will provide some short-term benefits to some renters. But these measures discourage investment in rental housing. Many owners will sell their properties and others will simply decide to refrain from investing in real estate. The expenses and hassles of meeting government mandates is more than many individuals are willing to endure. And a large percentage of rental property is owned by "mom-and-pop" operators—they own a small number of rental properties. Government controls are driving them from the industry.

Housing advocates frequently complain about the growing corporate presence in rental housing. These businesses recognize the profit potential of rental housing and have the capital to invest. More importantly, they have the resources to deal with the restrictions imposed by government. They have economies of scale that a "mom-and-pop" operation doesn't. In their zeal to protect tenants today, housing activists are advocating policies that contribute to the very thing they decry. If they considered the full context, if they looked at the long-term, they could see this. But the long-term isn't their concern. Nor is the long-term a concern for the advocates of rent control.

RENT CONTROL

The Swedish economist Assar Lindbeck once noted, "Next to bombing, rent control seems in many cases to be the most efficient technique so far known for destroying cities." Though there is not universal agreement among economists regarding rent control's destructive qualities, it is the one issue on which the majority of economists concur. In a survey of economists, 81 percent agreed that rent controls had a negative "impact over the past three decades on the amount and quality of broadly affordable rental housing in cities that have used them."[83]

Despite this, rent control is experiencing renewed popularity. Some of this can be attributed to the increased demands for tenant protections, and rent control certainly protects tenants from significant increases in rent. However, the advocates of rent control do not consider the full context. They look only at the short-term benefits to some tenants and ignore the long-term harm caused to landlords and other renters. Founded on the Progressive framework, rent control makes individuals subservient to the group.

Price Controls Create Shortages

Under rent control, government officials establish the maximum rents that a landlord can charge. Though the details vary, most rent control laws allow landlords to raise rents a small percentage (3 percent is typical) under certain conditions. But regardless of the details, rent control is a form of price control.

The purpose of rent control is to keep rents below the

level that would be charged in a free market. If we allow the market to operate freely, the argument goes, then developers and landlords will raise prices far beyond the affordability of most people. Rent control keeps housing affordable.

However, rent control, like all price controls, also has two negative consequences. When prices are held below their market value, individuals will buy more of the item—it's a deal. The second negative consequence is the discouragement of additional production.

The first point is simply a consequence of supply and demand. Stores reduce prices when they are trying to sell particular items, and they generally have an abundant supply. They use a lower price to increase demand, and they are prepared for it. When consumers discover a sale, many will buy more than they immediately need. Or, they may buy something that that they wouldn't purchase if it were not on sale. In either case, the lower price increases demand.

Price controls essentially force a business to hold a sale regardless of its supply or its desires. Just like a voluntary sale, price controls increase demand. However, if the business does not have an adequate supply, the artificially increased demand will quickly reduce the available stock. If the supply cannot be quickly increased, a shortage develops. However, because of the lower prices imposed by the controls, manufacturers of the product are not incentivized to increase production because their profit potential is artificially limited. The same principle applies to rent control and housing.

Where rent control exists, the demand for housing subject to those restrictions increases—that housing is on sale. Those who are fortunate enough to find a vacant rent-controlled apartment have little incentive to move in the future, even if their housing needs change. They are getting a good deal, and if they move, they will likely have to pay much higher rents. As a result, the turnover in rental housing is much lower when rent control is present. Some shoppers hoard when they find a good sale; some renters hoard when they find a rent-controlled apartment.

The result of this is that a housing shortage develops. Rent control increases demand for certain housing, while simultaneously discouraging the production of more housing. Even when new construction is excluded from rent control, housing producers know that their property could become subject to price controls in the future as the property ages or the law changes.

Developers and housing providers want to earn a return based on their productive abilities, not the dictates of government officials. By arbitrarily limiting the profit potential through rent control, developers and housing providers are incentivized to seek a better use for their investment capital. When it becomes less profitable or even unprofitable to own rental property, housing providers will move their capital to more profitable endeavors.

Rent control often includes other tenant protections, such as "just cause" eviction laws and the right to renew. Like the tenant protections we examined in the last chapter, rent control benefits some at the expense of others. The tenants who are able to locate a rent-controlled apartment benefit by paying below-market rates. However, other renters are unable to find housing at any price. And if the incumbent tenant seeks new housing in the future, he will probably find that he too has limited options. In the short-term, rent control provides the benefit of lower rent for some renters. In the long-term, rent control harms both tenants and landlords.

The Consequences Of Rent Control

The theoretical points made above have been proven by numerous case studies of cities with rent control, including San Francisco. In 1979, city officials in San Francisco imposed rent control on all apartment buildings with five or more units. A ballot initiative in 1994 expanded rent control to all multi-family housing.

In 2018, researchers looked at the impact of rent control in San Francisco. They found that the housing stock had dropped by 15 percent, even though demand was increasing. Much of the decrease was attributed to the conversion of apartment buildings to condominiums and thereby removed from the rental market. This is precisely what could have been predicted. Investors seek the best return on their capital, and when rent control limits that return, they seek other investments.

In addition, the conversions tended to be higher end and unaffordable to low- and moderate-income families. The new apartment construction that did occur also tended to be higher end. Not only did the overall supply of rental housing decrease, that which did exist was more expensive.

Other studies have found that the supply of rental units in Cambridge and Brookline, Massachusetts declined by 8 percent and 12 percent in the 1980s after stringent rent control laws were enacted.[84] In California, rent control reduced the housing supply by 14 percent in Berkeley and 8 percent in Santa Monica between 1978 and 1990, while in nearby cities without rent control the supply increased.[85] In the United Kingdom, rent control was imposed after World War II. The supply of privately owned rental housing dropped from 53 percent in 1950 to less than 8 percent in 1986.[86]

Cambridge provides an interesting example of rent control. A referendum in Massachusetts eliminated rent control throughout the state in 1994. While rent control was in place, rents for controlled units were typically 40 percent lower than comparable, uncontrolled units. In the twenty years after rent control ended, decontrolled properties appreciated 45 percent. One study that looked at Cambridge, found that property values in Cambridge increased by $2 billion between 1994 and 2004. But only $300 million was in the decontrolled units. The authors concluded that "the effect of rent control had been to reduce the whole neighborhood's desirability."[87] While the landlord is the immediate and obvious victim of rent control, all property owners suffer.

Rebecca Diamond, an Associate Professor of Economics at Stanford, notes that despite moving in different directions on rent control, San Francisco and Cambridge both experienced higher property values.

> It may seem surprising that the expansion of rent control in San Francisco led to an upgraded housing stock, catering to high-income tastes, while the removal of rent control in Cambridge also lead to upgrading and value appreciation. To reconcile these effects, it is useful to think about which types of landlords would respond to a rent control expansion versus a rent control removal.[88]

She goes on to explain that when rent control is imposed, many landlords will convert their building to condos or redevelop the building to exempt it from rent control. Such conversions generally target higher-income households, resulting in upgraded housing. When rent control is removed, landlords can increase their profits by upgrading their properties because they can increase rents to recover their investment. In both instances, landlords are driven by the profit motive, and they seek the tactic that will maximize their profits.

Another study looked at the mobility of tenants in San Francisco. The study looked at two types of renters—those who lived in rent-controlled buildings and those who didn't. The study found that those in rent-controlled buildings were 19 percent less likely to move than those who were in market-rate buildings.[89] Again, they are getting a good deal, and moving would subject them to much higher housing costs.

Despite the overwhelming evidence that rent control depletes the housing stock for low- and moderate-income families, calls for more rent control abound.

More Rent Control

In 2019, Oregon, California, and New York all enacted statewide rent control laws. In 2021, voters in St. Paul approved the nation's most stringent rent control law. Bernie Sanders has called for national rent control. The reason for this renewed popularity, according to Cea Weaver, the campaign coordinator of Housing Justice for All, is because rent control "works."

Whether a policy works or not depends on what one is trying to accomplish. According to Weaver,

> By curbing excessive rent hikes and preventing retaliatory or unjust eviction, rent control mitigates the power imbalance between tenants and landlords, advances overall neighborhood stability and prevents an eviction crisis as our cities become more expensive places to live.[90]

Weaver is correct that rent control curbs "excessive" increases in rent and prevents evictions. But she doesn't explain what an "excessive" increase is and why imposing price controls is just.

In a free market, an economic trade is based on the voluntary consent of each party. Each party is willing to trade one value for another. This is an act of justice, of granting to others that which they have earned. The trade is voluntary and mutually beneficial. However, under rent control, a landlord is forced to accept less than he would voluntarily choose. He does not receive a commensurate value for his trade.

To illustrate the essence of rent control consider a tenant who paid his rent and then demanded a partial refund at gunpoint. We would recognize his action as armed robbery. The principle does not change simply because government acts as the tenant's proxy and demands the refund up front. Rent control, like armed robbery, is an injustice, but "housing justice" activists aren't really concerned about justice. They are concerned only with getting benefits today, and they seek to use government coercion to obtain them.

When housing activists talk about balancing power, they evade the essence of the landlord/tenant trade. The landlord has a value that the tenant desires, and in many cities the demand for rental housing greatly exceeds the supply. This certainly gives the landlord a bargaining advantage, but tenants remain free to accept or reject his terms. However, housing activists don't want a voluntary trade. They want landlords to provide housing on terms set by tenants and their political supporters. They want individuals to be subservient to the group.

"The real goal of rent control," says Joshua Mason, an economics professor at Roosevelt University, "is protecting the moral rights of occupancy. Long-term tenants who have contributed to this being a desirable place to live have a legitimate interest in staying in their apartment."[91] In other words, since a tenant has a legitimate interest in staying in an apartment, he has a right to force the landlord to accept a lower rent. This argument, which is common, completely drops the context.

Tenants certainly have a moral right of occupancy, so long as they are abiding by the terms and conditions established in the agreement with the property's owner. That occupancy right is granted by the owner as a part of the trade between landlord and tenant. However, if at the end of the lease the landlord decides to raise the rent or change other terms of the lease, the tenant can accept the new offer, negotiate terms more to his liking, or move. He may not like his options, but no coercion is involved. If the tenant does not agree to a new lease, he forfeits his right to occupancy.

Landlords do not raise rents arbitrarily. The costs associated with a vacancy seldom makes a huge rent increase financially beneficial. For example, I have long-term tenants who are paying $150 to $200 a month less than comparable properties. If I increased the rent $150 per month, I would have increased my revenues by $1,800 over the course of a year. However, if the tenant cannot afford the new rent and must move, I could lose a month or more of rent while the property is vacant. I would also have the costs of cleaning, painting, utilities, and lawn maintenance. In total, a vacancy typically costs me more than $3,000. If my tenant moved because of a $150 increase, it would take twenty months to recover the make ready costs. I seldom raise the rents significantly.

Defenders of rent control believe that a tenant should be able to stay in an apartment as long as he chooses, regardless of the property owner's choices. They believe that the rent is too "damn high," and are willing to use government coercion to keep the rent artificially lower.

The Seen And The Unseen

The premise underlying rent control is that might makes right. Tenants vastly outnumber landlords, and they exert considerable pressure to enact laws that benefit them. As one example, in St. Paul, the majority of voters imposed their desires on the minority—landlords. That rent control was enacted by a majority does not change the principle. Unlimited majority rule empowers the majority to do anything it chooses simply because it is the majority. This is the Progressive framework in action.

Majority rule enables the group to impose its values upon individuals. However, truth and justice are not determined by a vote.

In enacting rent control, both voters and politicians are looking only at the short-term benefits. However, as Henry Hazlett writes in *Economics in One Lesson*, "But if we have trained ourselves to look beyond immediate to secondary consequences, and beyond those who are directly benefited by a government project to others who are indirectly affected, a different picture presents itself."[92] Unfortunately, this type of analysis seldom occurs.

The beneficiaries of rent control are easy to identify and see. But the victims of rent control—landlords and other renters—are unseen. If we want to make good policy decisions, then we must look at the long-term consequences. We must consider the full context.

Considering the full context is neither easy nor automatic. Holding context requires concerted, and often prolonged, mental effort. If we refuse to exert that effort, we will not make the best decisions possible. And that means that we won't solve the affordable housing crisis or achieve housing justice.

SUBSIDIES FOR RENTAL HOUSING

Housing subsidies are used for both tenants and homeowners. We will focus on rental subsidies in this chapter. There are five primary subsidy programs: public housing, Housing Choice Vouchers, Section 8 project-based, supportive elderly and disabled, and USDA Rural Rental Assistance. More than five million households receive some form of rental subsidy with public housing and Housing Choice Vouchers accounting for nearly two-thirds of those receiving rental subsidies.

According to Investopedia,

> A subsidy is a benefit given to an individual, business, or institution, usually by the government. It can be direct (such as cash payments) or indirect (such as tax breaks). The subsidy is typically given to remove some type of burden, and it is often considered to be in the overall interest of the public, given to promote a social good or an economic policy.[93]

In other words, subsidies are given because there is some perceived benefit to the public—the group.

Subsidies for rental housing remove some of the financial burden that low-income families face and ostensibly help them obtain decent, affordable housing. However, these programs do nothing to increase the supply of housing for low-income households.

Public Housing

The Housing Act of 1937 authorized the federal government to begin building public housing projects. Twelve years later, another act authorized the construction of 810,000 units of public housing. At the time the law was passed, President Harry Truman said the bill

> opens up the prospect of decent homes in wholesome surroundings for low-income families now living in the squalor of the slums. It equips the Federal Government, for the first time, with effective means for aiding cities in the vital task of clearing slums and rebuilding blighted areas. This legislation permits us to take a long step toward increasing the well-being and happiness of millions of our fellow citizens. Let us not delay in fulfilling that high purpose.

That high purpose soon turned into an abject failure. Many housing projects were built in conjunction with slum clearance. Hundreds, and sometimes thousands, of affordable homes were demolished to make room for high-rises and other multi-family housing, as well as non-housing developments. During the 1950s, more than 425,000 homes were demolished, but public housing projects replaced only 125,000. Truman's grand promises never came true.

One of the most infamous of the high-rise projects was the Pruitt-Igoe development in St. Louis, Missouri. Built in 1955 and 1956 the project had 2,870 units in thirty-three high rise buildings. Designed by Minoru Yamasaki, Pruitt-Igoe was intended to be the flagship for removing tenements and modernizing the nation's cities. Yamasaki believed that good intentions and strong central government planning would enable a society to progress. His designs were sold as the solution to poverty, crime, and housing in America's largest cities. Further, it was argued that if people lived in a decent home, rather than a tenement, the "common good" would somehow be served.

Construction of Pruitt-Igoe was funded by government. On paper, rents received from tenants would pay the operating and maintenance costs, and the project would be self-supporting. However, like many similar government schemes, the reality was much different. Many of the tenants were unemployed, rather than working poor. It quickly became apparent that the rents being paid were insufficient to properly maintain the buildings.

In addition, at the time Missouri law only allowed single parents to receive welfare, so many poor families faced the choice of forgoing that entitlement or living apart. Many fathers left their families. With less parental attention, many children joined gangs and began vandalizing the buildings. The gangs were soon terrorizing residents as well.

The buildings had been designed with wide hallways and elevators that only stopped on every third floor. The goal was to encourage socializing and foster a sense of community. However, the elevators became, as Amity Shlaes put it in *Great Society*, "muggers' traps"[94] and the hallways were a gauntlet that residents had to maneuver to safely reach their home.

By the late 1960s, vacancy rates in the project reached as high as 65%, and Pruitt-Igoe was known around the world for its poverty and crime. By 1971, only six-hundred people lived in the complex's 2,780 apartments and sixteen of the buildings had been boarded up. In only fifteen years, Pruitt-Igoe went from the showcase project for urban renewal to a symbol of poverty, crime, and misery—the very things that the public housing project was supposed to eliminate. The buildings were demolished between 1972 and 1975. This pattern of deteriorating buildings and crime was repeated in public housing projects across the nation. The Housing and Urban Development Act of 1969 shifted the style of public housing away from high-rises, which many concluded concentrated poverty and were unsuitable for families with children. The failure of Pruitt-Igoe demonstrate that good intentions do not necessarily make for good policy.

Public housing projects soon fell into disrepute as maintenance suffered and crime proliferated. In 1974, President Nixon placed a moratorium on new public housing projects and the government began to depend more on the private housing market. The Faircloth Amendment in the late 1990s prohibited an increase in the number of public housing units. Since that time, the number of public housing units has remained around one million. However, a number of Congressmen are working to repeal the Faircloth Amendment and set the stage for a new round of advocacy for public housing.

Public Housing, Redux

President Biden has proposed $40 billion to renovate the nation's public housing. Senate Majority Leader Chuck Schumer has demanded $80 billion for the same purpose. Sen Bernie Sanders and Rep. Alexandria Ocasio-Cortez introduced the Green New Deal for Public Housing Act. The act calls for the government to spend $172 billion to renovate every public housing unit in the nation to be more energy efficient. Not to be outdone, Rep. Ilhan Omar has proposed spending $800 billion to build 9.5 million new public housing units.

When Sanders and Cortez announced their bill, the Senator said,

> It is unacceptable that over half a million people in America, the richest country on Earth, are homeless. It is unacceptable that for so many working people it is incredibly hard to find affordable housing. It is unacceptable that our nation's public housing is in a state of chronic disrepair and energy inefficiency after generations of government neglect.[95]

Ocasio-Cortez noted, "Just to address the backlog of critical maintenance repairs in NYCHA [New York City Housing Authority] and nowhere else – chipping lead paint, broken heating systems, failing gas utilities – would require $40M...."[96]

While acknowledging that public housing has suffered

from government neglect for decades, the two members of Congress make no mention of how they will avoid a repeat of that in the future. Instead, they will deal with the immediate problem by throwing a boatload of taxpayer money at it. The long-term consequences aren't their concern—they want today's problem fixed today. This is what occurs when one looks at an issue in isolation and does not consider the full context. This type of out-of-context policy analysis is what happens when one embraces the Progressive framework.

Sanders and Ocasio-Cortez claim that their bill will create nearly 250,000 well-paying construction jobs. Those jobs will be immediate and easy to perceive. What isn't immediate and as easy to see are the jobs that will be lost.

Public works mean taxation, inflation (which economist Henry Hazlett called a vicious form of taxation), or both. A dollar of government spending means a dollar of taxation. The $172 billion that Sanders and Ocasio-Cortez propose to spend on public housing will benefit the two million residents of those units. The 250,000 jobs created will benefit those workers. These are the direct beneficiaries of the act. However, every dollar spent on public housing is a dollar taken away from taxpayers, who would have spent that money on other things and helped create other jobs. Using a bridge as his example, Hazlett concludes, "Therefore, for every public job created by the bridge project a private job has been destroyed somewhere else."[97] The jobs that are lost or not created are difficult to see.

Focused on the immediate and the easily perceived, advocates for public housing blind themselves to the broader long-term consequences of their policies. Money taken from taxpayers is money that those individuals can't spend on *their* housing, education for *their* children, and anything else *they* desire—spending that would have created or sustained jobs. But the unjust suffering imposed upon taxpayers and indirect victims is more difficult to identify and see. "The jobs destroyed by the taxes for housing," Hazlett writes in *Economics in One Lesson,* are not seen, nor the goods and services that were never made. It takes a concentrated effort of thought, and a new effort each time the houses and the happy people in them are seen, to think of the wealth that was not created instead.[98]

This concentrated effort of thought, the desire to look beyond the immediate and easily seen, is precisely what is missing from housing policy discussions. If we truly wish to solve the housing crisis, then we must reject this framework. We must look at the big picture—the full context. And that means looking beyond the immediate and easily seen. Of course, that is precisely what the Progressive framework regards as impossible.

Housing Choice Vouchers

The Housing Choice Voucher Program (sometimes called Section 8) was created in 1974 by an amendment to the Housing Act of 1937. Administered through the Department for Housing and Urban Development, the program was a part of the government's shift from public housing projects to a reliance on the private housing market.

Under the voucher program, local housing authorities are allotted a specific dollar amount for vouchers. The local officials collect and process applications, inspect properties, and disburse funds. Participants pay 30 percent of their income for housing, and the voucher programs pays the remaining rent.

In most jurisdictions, there is a years-long waiting list of applicants. An estimated 17.7 million households are eligible for the program, but funding is available for only 2.2 million. As a candidate, Biden proposed providing vouchers for every eligible household, a position he has since backed away from. However, he has proposed spending $5.4 billion each year to add 200,000 families to the program. Congressional Democrats have proposed expanding assistance to one-million households at an annual cost of $90 billion. Even if this grandiose plan is enacted, less than 20 percent of the eligible families will be in the program. To provide vouchers for every eligible family, the government would have to spend more than $1 trillion each year.

In 2018, the Congressional Budget Office noted that the voucher program is unfair because a small percentage of eligible households actually receive the subsidy. It is true that the program provides benefits to some low-income households while denying those benefits to other low-income households, but this isn't the fundamental reason the program is unfair. The program takes money from taxpayers to pay for the housing of others. That is the true injustice.

Expanding the voucher program means more than just allotting additional funds. An expanded program would require more bureaucrats at the Department for Housing and Urban Development, as well as at the local housing authorities. And, even if the program were expanded, many landlords do not accept housing vouchers, which is often called "source of income" discrimination.

Some housing activists call this a veiled form of racism. The majority of voucher users are "people of color," and activists claim that refusing to accept vouchers is just a cover for refusing to rent to blacks, Hispanics, and other minorities. Christina Rosales, deputy director of Texas Housers, an organization that advocates for renters, has said, "Saying that they don't accept vouchers is all a proxy for race."[99] Perhaps some landlords are racists, but such claims are a generalization that isn't supported by the facts.

If a landlord wishes to accept housing vouchers, his property is subjected to an inspection by local housing officials. The wait time for an inspection can be weeks. If the property fails the inspection, the owner must quickly make repairs and then schedule another inspection. Another failure stops the process, and the landlord must go to the back of the line.

The inspection per se is not an obstacle for most landlords. Many of the inspection standards are reasonable and easily met. For example, the inspection will ensure that lighting and outlets work, that there are no plumbing leaks or broken windows, and check that exterior doors have proper locks. However, other aspects of the inspection are not as reasonable. For example, an operational refrigerator and stove must be present at the time of inspection. But many landlords—myself included—do not provide these appliances because tenants abuse them. However, to pass the inspection and remain in the program, the landlord would have to incur the expense of buying a refrigerator and stove, as well as the costs for future maintenance and cleaning of those appliances.

Periodic inspections by housing authorities are used to verify that the property is being maintained. If they find problems, housing authorities can withhold payment to the landlords until the issue is resolved. Ian Mattingly, director of the Apartment Association of Greater Dallas, says, "I've seen apartments fail because of a hairline crack in a plastic faceplate over a light switch cover."[100] He calls the inspection process "highly subjective."[101]

When I first started investing in rental housing, I investigated the voucher program. I spoke with housing authorities, read their literature, and attended a seminar to learn more about the program. I decided against entering the program. In addition to the hassle of periodic and subjective inspections, it would take nearly two months from the time I applied until I could begin interviewing tenants. This would mean that the property would remain vacant and generate no income while the bureaucrats doddle. Given that I usually find a tenant within about two weeks, this was an unacceptable delay.

I do not want to endure the hassle and expense of dealing with a government bureaucracy in order to accept vouchers, and many landlords agree with me. For most landlords, the refusal to accept vouchers has nothing to do with race. It is worth noting that more than 90 percent of my tenants have been black or Hispanic. If my reason for refusing to accept vouchers is racism, then I am not a very consistent practitioner of that hideous creed.

But housing activists do not accept these facts. Following the Progressive framework, they refuse to consider the full context. They see landlords doing something that they don't like, and they want to compel landlords to act in a more agreeable manner. They want to force landlords to accept housing vouchers. A dozen states and many municipalities have made their wish come true by passing laws prohibiting source of income discrimination.

Activists argue that these laws give tenants the freedom to choose their housing. At the same time, these laws deny landlords the freedom to choose whether to accept vouchers or not. To advance freedom of choice for some while denying it to others is neither just nor morally defensible. Since housing advocates can't convince landlords to accept vouchers, they will resort to force to achieve what they failed to gain by voluntary means.

Again, we see that housing advocates examine the issue from a narrow perspective—the alleged benefit to tenants—while evading the impact on others. They look only at the immediate "benefit" while ignoring the long-term harm. When landlords are prohibited from acting as they judge best, many will simply get out of the rental housing business or remove their properties from the rental market. The supply of affordable housing will decrease further, and low-income individuals will have fewer options for housing

Criticisms Of Vouchers

Some housing activists are critical of many government housing policies, particularly vouchers, because they are "market centered." Proposals to expand the voucher program or offer more tax credits, they correctly argue, mirror past efforts that have failed. Activists Gianpaolo Baiocchi and H. Jacob Carlson write,

[T]he bulk of the proposals in the American Jobs Plan

[a Biden proposal], for example, mostly mirror earlier policies to stimulate ownership and new construction of affordable housing through subsidies and tax-breaks for private developers. These mechanisms have not only contributed to our problems, but failed African Americans.[102]

Baiocchi's and Carlson's primary objection to subsidies and tax credits is that they rely on the private market to supply affordable housing. The proper solution, they claim, is to remove housing from the private market.

These activists, along with many others, want to socialize housing and put government in complete control. Past public housing projects have proven that public housing is a disaster, but the activists aren't dissuaded. True to the Progressive framework, what happened in the past is no indication of what will happen in the future. And so, they propose variations of past policies and hope that somehow the future results will be different.

Citing the work of housing scholars, Baiocchi and Carlson make their essential point:

When these public goods and social necessities (what [one scholar] calls "fictitious commodities") are treated *as if* they are commodities produced for sale on the market, rather than protected rights, our social world is endangered and major crises will ensue.[103]

The alternative proposed by Baiocchi and Carlson is social (public) housing. "Social housing works," they write, "because it aligns the interests of residents with those of the collective. In contrast, private rental housing pits landlords against tenants in fights over costs and maintenance."[104] Not surprisingly, Baiocchi and Carlson hold the interests of the collective as the standard. And when the group is the standard, the "rights" of the group (tenants) will conflict with the rights of non-members (landlords and other individuals).

Nor is it surprising that they argue for democratic control of housing, which is simply a mechanism for the majority to impose its desires and values on others. "Social housing requires imagining a kind of housing whose production, distribution, and management is guided by deeply democratic principles, a logic of intentional inclusion, and an ethos of care and environmental stewardship."[105]

Social housing means subjugating the individual to the group. The group will vote on the production, distribution, and management of housing. Individuals will attain housing, not on the basis of their actions, but by securing enough votes from other members of the community. This isn't a plan for justice. It is a plan for mob rule. Whatever the majority decides is proper because it is the majority. Despite the history of poverty, crime, and misery associated with public housing, Baiocchi and Carlson want more of it.

Further, they want to give control of the production, distribution, and management of housing to individuals who have little or no experience in doing so. Few tenants have the skills to properly produce and manage housing developments. Giving untrained, non-experts control over housing is a recipe for a colossal failure.

Contrary to what activists claim, the nation's housing policies are not "market centered." Government intervention in housing abounds, and it has for more than a century. Zoning restricts the freedom of owners to build additional housing on a lot. Low-cost mortgages create an artificial demand for home ownership. Vouchers take money from taxpayers to subsidize the housing of others. Tax credits motivate developers and others to take actions that they would not do otherwise. Governments at every level have used prohibitions, mandates, and manipulation to control and regulate the production, distribution, and management of housing. That is not a market-centered approach, and it is intellectually dishonest to claim otherwise.

Ignoring government's massive intervention in housing markets, activists claim that the present housing shortage is a consequence of the free market. Such claims are disingenuous at best. We will not make the best possible decisions if we do not consider the full context. We cannot solve the housing crisis if we misrepresent the facts.

Subsidies Beget Dependency

An old proverb holds that if you give a man a fish, you will allow him to eat today. But if you teach him to fish, he can eat every day. Giving him a fish makes him dependent on others for tomorrow's sustenance. Teaching him to fish makes him independent. Housing advocates want to give low-income households a fish, rather than enabling them to produce and flourish.

Subsidies provide short-term relief by relieving an individual's financial burden today. But subsidies do nothing to enable him to prosper tomorrow. And, if an individual comes to rely on housing subsidies, his motivation to improve his financial situation is curtailed. He becomes dependent on the subsidies. To understand this, one must consider the full context. However, the Progressive framework demands that we ignore the full context.

If we want low-income households to flourish and attain the housing that they desire, we must enable them to do so through their own efforts. We must enable them to be independent.

SUBSIDIES FOR HOMEOWNERSHIP

For nearly a century, government officials have believed that home ownership is inherently good, and government must make it easier for Americans to own a home. Since the 1930s, the federal government has actively sought to encourage home ownership through a variety of subsidies. That policy continues to this day. The Federal Housing Administration, the Department of Housing and Urban Development, Fannie Mae, and Freddie Mac are the primary entities providing subsidies for homeowners.

Since the 1970s, the federal government has attempted to overcome the racist housing policies of the past with a myriad of programs and policies intended to make it easier for minorities to buy a house. Two examples are policies that we previously examined—the Community Reinvestment Act and Andrew Cuomo's 1999 directive that Fannie Mae and Freddie Mac provide more support for low- and moderate-income families to obtain a home mortgage.

The destruction wrought by those policies hasn't dissuaded housing advocates and their political supporters from advocating policies that are just a variation on the theme. Founded on the Progressive framework, those policies will ultimately have the same destructive consequences.

New Fhfa Goals For Gses

The Federal Housing Finance Agency (FHFA) was created in 2008 following the Great Recession. Its purpose is to regulate the government-sponsored enterprises (GSEs) Fannie Mae and Freddie Mac, as well as eleven Federal Home Loan Banks. In 2021, the FHFA issued new goals for the GSEs regarding loans to minorities and low-income households. From 2022 to 2024 the two mortgage giants must ensure that 10 percent of their loans are for properties in minority census tracts and 4 percent must be in low-income census tracts. Similar to Cuomo's directive, these new goals will make more funds available in low-income and minority neighborhoods.

Previous goals targeted low-income neighborhoods without regard to race or demographics, a policy that some claim reinforced existing disparities in the housing market. Nikitra Bailey, senior vice president of public policy at the National Fair Housing Alliance, said, "Whites and Asian borrowers are overrepresented in the underserved market that the GSE's are targeting."[106] One of the keys, she added, is ensuring that funds help the people that they are meant to help, i.e., "people of color." FHFA policies after the Great Recession, Bailey noted, had a "disproportionate impact on Black and brown families." Bailey went on to claim, "We have the chance to grow the economy by a trillion dollars a year. It makes sense to make sure these families can have access to the mortgages they desire because the health of the overall market will depend on how they are served." In other words, the future health of the economy depends upon satisfying the desires of this particular group.

Government officials made similar predictions. FHFA acting director at the time, Sandra L. Thompson, said, "The Enterprises' housing goals over the next three years should support equitable access to sustainable affordable housing opportunities in a safe and sound manner that bolsters the health of communities." She didn't explain how making risky loans to individuals with low incomes and poor credit scores is safe and sound.

These words echo Andrew Cuomo's claims when he announced new goals for the GSEs in 1999.

> This action will transform the lives of millions of families across our country by giving them new opportunities to buy homes or move into apartments with rents they can afford. It will strengthen our economy and create jobs by stimulating more home construction, it will help ease the terrible shortage of affordable housing plaguing far too many communities, and it will help reduce the huge homeownership gap dividing whites from minorities and suburbs from cities.[107]

Focusing on a different group doesn't change the essence of this new policy. Rather than targeting one group —low-income families—the new goals target another group—minorities. And, while bureaucrats continue to issue grand promises about rebuilding communities, these policies, like Cuomo's, will ultimately have destructive consequences.

While denouncing past housing policies based on skin color, the FHFA has set new goals based on skin color. Such race-based policies are founded on "good intentions." However, good intentions alone do not lead to good results. One must also have good policies. However, good policies are nearly impossible when one embraces the Progressive framework and drops the context.

As in the 2000s, extending more loans in "underserved" communities will ultimately require lowering underwriting standards. There is a reason that these individuals are "underserved"—they are not a good credit risk. The financial position of the individuals within the targeted groups has not improved since the early 2000s. Indeed, many housing advocates note that the financial position of minorities has declined since the Great Recession. Many, if not most, of these individuals still have poor credit histories. They still lack the savings required to make a down payment. There is no rational reason to believe that the results of increasing loans to these individuals will be any different from the 2000s. The details may differ, but the principle does not because the framework hasn't changed. We are supposed to believe that somehow the results will be different this time.

This new effort to increase home ownership among minorities isn't the only program that provides subsidies for home ownership.

Neighborhood Homes Investment Act

The Neighborhood Homes Investment Act (NHIA) is similar to the Low-Income Housing Tax Credit. However, where the Low-Income Housing Tax Credit is used to support rental housing, NHIA supports owner-occupied housing.

In neighborhoods with poorly maintained homes, it is difficult to attract the capital for new home construction or substantial rehabilitation of homes. Proponents of the bill claimed that NHIA

> would break this stalemate by creating a federal tax credit that covers the gap between the cost of building or renovating homes and the price at which they can be sold, thus making renovation and new home construction possible. The NHIA would also help existing homeowners in these neighborhoods to rehabilitate their homes.[108]

The program targets communities with high poverty rates, low median family incomes, and low home values. About 22 percent of urban census tracts and 27 percent of non-urban census tracts qualify for NHIA tax credits.

Like the Low-Income Housing Tax Credit, NHIA tax credits are allocated to the states, which then disburse the credits and monitor compliance with the program's terms and conditions. About two billion dollars in tax credits has been authorized by the act.

The program has significant restrictions on homes that are newly built or substantially rehabilitated for sale. Purchasers cannot have an income above 140 percent of the area/state median income. Sales prices are limited to four times the area or state median family income. Tax credits are issued for the difference between development costs and the sales price required by the program.

Tax credits for rehabilitation by a current owner-occupant have similar restrictions. The homeowner must have an income at or below the area/state median income. The tax credits cannot exceed $50,000. If the homeowner sells the property within five years, he must repay a percentage of the tax credit ranging from 50 percent in the first year to 10 percent in year five.

The act's sponsors project that 500,000 homes will be built or substantially rehabilitated over ten years. Nearly 800,000 jobs will be created with combined wages and salaries of about $43 million. This act, like the FHFA's new goals for the GSEs, is accompanied with great fanfare and grand promises. But great fanfare and grand promises do not make good policy.

The National Council of State Housing Agency, an advocate of the act, notes that private investors would not finance affordable housing without an incentive like the NHIA tax credit

> because the numbers simply do not work without the NHIA tax credit. No investor will spend more money to purchase a vacant lot/abandoned home/home in need of substantial rehab and invest the time and money to undertake the work than they can get back from that property's sale. It just doesn't make economic sense without the NHIA tax credit.[109]

Rather than address the reasons why the numbers don't work without tax credits, politicians use the credits to incentivize/bribe private investors and companies to take actions they otherwise wouldn't. Some will benefit from this program, but it doesn't address the fundamental cause of the problem. The high cost of new housing is accepted as an immutable fact, and the only alternatives considered are subsidies in one form or another.

The Progressive framework demands that we look only at the immediate and easily seen results. It demands that we ignore the long-term consequences and the less easily seen. Certainly, NHIA will create easily seen jobs, but we will never know how many unseen jobs will be destroyed in the process.

Affirmatively Furthering Fair Housing

In 2015, HUD approved a rule known as Affirmatively Furthering Fair Housing. The purpose of the rule was to speed the pace of housing integration by requiring municipalities receiving federal funds for housing or urban development to document patterns or practices of racial bias and to create a plan to rectify those barriers.

The municipalities were required to analyze housing occupancy by race, disability, familial status, economic status, and numerous other categories. If patterns of racial bias were discovered, the municipality had to submit a plan to HUD to remedy the situation. And if that plan was deemed unacceptable, federal funds would be withheld.

Municipalities quickly discovered that the reporting requirements consumed exorbitant amounts of resources. Responding to complaints from municipalities, the Trump Administration suspended the rule in January 2018, and then terminated it in July 2020. The HUD Secretary at the time, Ben Carson, said, "After reviewing thousands of comments on the proposed changes to the Affirmatively Furthering Fair Housing (AFFH) regulation, we found it to be unworkable and ultimately a waste of time for localities to comply with, too often resulting in funds being steered away from communities that need them most."[110] In a tweet, Trump wrote,

I am happy to inform all of the people living their Suburban

> Lifestyle Dream that you will no longer be bothered or financially hurt by having low income housing built in your neighborhood.... Your housing prices will go up based on the market, and crime will go down. I have rescinded the Obama-Biden AFFH Rule. Enjoy![111]

Within months of taking office, Biden's Administration announced that the rule would be reinstated. However, the "unnecessarily burdensome" reporting requirements would be removed.

Promoting racial and economic integration is just as bad of a government policy as promoting racial and economic segregation. Government should be neutral the issue. But that hasn't been the case for decades.

Beginning in the 1930s, government actively promoted and enacted policies designed to create racial and economic segregation. Exclusionary zoning was promoted by the federal government, enacted on the local level, and ultimately sanctioned by the Supreme Court. The FHA and VA both discriminated against blacks because of their skin color. Federal highway policy has often targeted low-income and minority neighborhoods for demolition to expand freeways. More recently, government has actively promoted and enacted policies designed to create racial and economic integration. Whether for exclusion or for inclusion, for one hundred years government housing policies have been largely based on race. This is what is required by the Progressive framework that has dominated policy discussions.

Downpayment Toward Equity Act

In July 2021, Rep. Maxine Waters introduced the Downpayment Toward Equity Act of 2021. The program would provide grants to the states to use for down payment assistance for "first-generation" homebuyers. The act authorizes $100 billion over ten years for the program. To be eligible for the program, a state must have adopted a plan to affirmatively further fair housing.

To qualify for the program, a home buyer must have an income at or below 120 percent of the area median income. Those who have owned a home in the previous three years, or whose parents or guardians currently own a home, or whose spouse has owned a home in the previous three years are not eligible.

The program provides up to $20,000 in assistance, and up to $25,000 for homebuyers who qualify as a "socially and economically disadvantaged individual." A FAQ sheet published by the Nation Council of State Housing Agencies, states,

> The Act defines "socially disadvantaged individuals" as "those who have been subjected to racial or ethnic prejudice or cultural bias because of their identity as a member of a group without regard to their individual qualities."
>
> Any individual identifying as black, Hispanic, Asian American, Native American or any combination thereof, will be presumed to meet this definition. Any individual who does not identify as such will have to prove by the preponderance of evidence that they are socially disadvantaged."[112]

Individuals will receive a greater subsidy if they are a member of certain racial/ethnic groups. Such individuals, the act presumes, have been subjected to prejudice or bias "without regard to their individual qualities." This means that eligibility for the program is determined by membership in a group rather than "individual qualities." The act itself ignores "individual qualities" and is prejudiced against individuals who aren't a member of a preferred group.

As with FHA and VA loans after World War II, the Downpayment Toward Equity Act of 2021 is a racist policy. Individuals are to be judged for eligibility, not on the basis of their own "individual qualities," but by their skin color. It was an injustice when the FHA and VA did it, and it is an injustice if HUD does it.

The program will help some individuals purchase a home, just as the subprime loans of the early 2000s helped many buy a home. Accumulating enough money for a down payment is one of the biggest obstacles to purchasing a home. This program will overcome that challenge. However, the cost of owning a home is far more than coming up with a down payment and paying the mortgage. A homeowner must pay utilities, repairs and maintenance, insurance, and property taxes

If a family is unable to save the money for a down payment, will they be able to save enough money to pay for the inevitable and necessary repairs? A new roof or HVAC system can easily cost $7,000. A water heater can cost $1,200 or more. Paying for such repairs can be financially devastating. And if a homeowner is unable to pay for these repairs, the condition of the house will deteriorate along with its value. Medical bills or automobile repairs can also add unexpected expenses.

Further, if an individual sells the house within the first year, he must repay the assistance he received. The repayment decreases 20 percent each year, and after five years no repayment must be made if the house is sold. Again, if a family was unable to save the money in the first place, they are not likely going to save the money to repay the assistance that they received if they sell early.

Owning a home is more expensive than renting. Lending Tree, an online lending marketplace, compared the cost of renting versus home ownership in the nations fifty largest metropolitan areas. The company found that homeowners with a mortgage pay $606 more than renters.[113] Programs like this might seem laudable because they help individuals buy a home. But these programs can also be setting individuals up for colossal financial problems.

Looking at the long-term consequences of a policy is precisely what the Progressive framework disdains. And so, policies that are destructive in the long-term are announced with grand promises and great fanfare.

Miscellaneous Programs

The Unlocking Possibilities Program provides $1.75 billion in grants to states, local governments, and Native American tribes to "improve and implement housing plans and strategies."[114] One supporter of the program is Up for Growth, a coalition whose "mission is to forge policies and partnerships to achieve housing equity, eliminate systemic barriers, and create more homes."[115]

The organization writes that the Unlocking Possibilities Program

> will provide communities with resources to develop housing needs assessments and design and implement policies to eliminate exclusionary zoning and artificial barriers to boost production of needed homes, particularly in areas where the most significant imbalances exist between the number of jobs and the amount of available housing.[116]

Eliminating exclusionary zoning and artificial barriers to the production of housing are laudable goals. However, the federal government does not need to spend a single penny to design and implement policies to do so. What is needed is simply to repeal those laws that restrict the production and consumption of housing. Repealing laws doesn't cost anything. However, repealing laws does not provide political favors to the favored group. Consequently, repealing laws isn't an alternative that is considered.

The HOME Investment Partnerships Program (HOME) provides block grants to states and local jurisdictions to fund a range of housing activities, including building or rehabilitating affordable housing for low-income households. According to the website for the Department of Housing and Urban Development, which funds the program, "The program's flexibility allows states and local governments to use HOME funds for grants, direct loans, loan guarantees or other forms of credit enhancements, or rental assistance or security deposits."[117]

The Good Neighbor Next Door Program offers law enforcement officers, teachers, firefighters, and emergency medical technicians a 50 percent discount on single-family homes. The homes are selected by the Department of Housing and Urban Development (HUD) and are located in "revitalization areas." HUD acquires the homes through foreclosure on a loan insured by the Federal Housing Administration (FHA). This limits the number of homes that are available.

Home buyers are required to sign a second "silent" mortgage at closing. If the buyer remains in the home for three years, HUD releases its mortgage. Buyers with a credit score above 580 are eligible for maximum financing, while those with a credit score between 500 and 579 are limited to 90 percent of the property's value.

Like the loans insured by the FHA and the Veterans Administration (VA) in the post-war years, the Good Neighbor Next Door Program provides benefits to some Americans while excluding others. Just as the FHA and the VA provided mortgages for one group—whites—the Good Neighbor Next Door Program provides mortgages for other groups. It was wrong for the FHA and VA to exclude those who were not in the preferred group, and it is wrong for HUD to do so.

The More Things Change

Changing the details of a policy does not modify its essence. The current programs and proposals are simply variations on past policies. They remain subsidies that are targeted at one group or another.

The same cause has the same effect. In the early 2000s, low-income households were targeted for home ownership subsidies. Twenty years later, government officials are repeating that disastrous policy. The results will be similar—unqualified individuals will buy a home, only to later discover that they cannot afford home ownership.

Government does individuals no favors when it subsidizes home ownership. It simply encourages actions that would otherwise not occur. It encourages actions that are often harmful in the long-term. But if one looks only at the short-term benefits—increased home ownership for a targeted group—the long-term is irrelevant. That has been the dominant framework for more than a century, and it remains the dominant framework today.

GENTRIFICATION

Across the nation, controversy rages over gentrification, pitting long-time residents of a neighborhood against new residents and developers. Some argue that gentrification is good because it revitalizes impoverished neighborhoods. Others argue that it is a destructive process that tears communities apart and changes a neighborhood's character.

Despite the strong opinions and heated discussions about gentrification, commentators and activists define the concept differently. Indeed, The National Low Income Housing Coalition acknowledges, "There are many definitions for gentrification, which can make discussions about development and displacement confusing."[118] So, before we can examine policies related to gentrification, we should first identify what the concept truly means.

What Is Gentrification?

The website for the University of Texas states that,

> Gentrification is a process of neighborhood change where higher-income and higher-educated residents move into a historically marginalized neighborhood, housing costs rise, and the neighborhood is physically transformed through new higher-end construction and building upgrades, resulting in the displacement of vulnerable residents and changes to the neighborhood's cultural character.[119]

The Urban Displacement Project defines gentrification as

> a process of neighborhood change that includes economic change in a historically disinvested neighborhood —by means of

real estate investment and new higher-income residents moving in – as well as demographic change – not only in terms of income level, but also in terms of changes in the education level or racial make-up of residents.[120]

The National Low Income Housing Coalition offers another definition.

> Many anti-displacement activists define gentrification as a profit-driven, race, and class change of a historically disinvested neighborhood. "Disinvested" in this context means areas that businesses and governments have abandoned—where there has been little new development or maintenance of existing buildings or institutions. Gentrification occurs where land is cheap and the chance to make a profit is high due to the influx of wealthier wage earners willing to pay higher rents.[121]

While these definitions differ in some details, they agree that gentrification is a process that transforms an impoverished neighborhood. That transformation occurs when developers and businesses invest money to upgrade or build new housing, restaurants, and retail shops. As this occurs, wealthier individuals are attracted to the neighborhood and its racial and economic character often begins to change.

Most gentrification occurs in neighborhoods near the central city. These areas have often been neglected for decades by both the public and private sectors. Deteriorating infrastructure, dilapidated housing, impoverishment, and few economic opportunities are typical characteristics of neighborhoods that become targets for gentrification.

It is often said that the three most important things to consider when buying real estate are: location, location, and location. Proximity to the central city makes these neighborhoods increasingly attractive to a wide range of people who want to be close to entertainment, work, museums, and other amenities. They want to live in a "walkable community" where they are less dependent on an automobile. The location of these neighborhoods makes them attractive for redevelopment. It is, in a sense, an opportunity for the neighborhood to start anew.

In addition to their location, these impoverished neighborhoods generally have low property values, at least early in the gentrification process. The lower cost to acquire properties attracts and provides an incentive for developers, builders, businesses, and real estate investors to invest in a poor neighborhood because they anticipate that property values will eventually rise. As gentrification proceeds and demand for housing and other development in the neighborhood increases, so do property values.

It is important to realize that gentrification is not an organized effort. Dozens or perhaps hundreds of different individuals and businesses see an area as a good investment. Individually, their efforts have a small impact. However, together their efforts slowly transform a neighborhood from an impoverished neighborhood to a community bustling with economic activity. Many do not view this as a good thing and seek to stop gentrification.

Fighting Gentrification

Opponents of gentrification present three essential arguments against the process. These form the basis for much of the controversy over gentrification.

The first argument is that rents increase. When housing is upgraded through extensive rehabilitation or new construction, the owner can obtain a higher rent. As demand for housing in the neighborhood grows, this puts additional upward pressure on rents. Higher rents are often unaffordable to the incumbent residents who are generally low-income families, and many must relocate. They are, according to this argument, displaced.

While many believe that gentrification leads to higher rents, numerous recent studies have found differently. Researchers at UCLA's Lewis Center for Regional Policy Studies examined six different studies that looked at the impact of new market-rate housing on the rents in a gentrifying neighborhood. Five of the six studies found that new development tempers rent increases rather than accelerate them. One of those studies focused on San Francisco and found that rents within one-hundred meters of new market-rate housing rents decreased 2 percent. Further, the risk of displacement for low-income renters decreased by 17 percent.[122]

Michael Manville, an urban planning professor at UCLA says that the reason is that new construction eases demand for the existing housing.

> Do you want newer residents moving in and displacing residents in the existing housing? Or do you want them to be in brand new housing where, while they will change the neighborhood by their presence, they don't put as much pressure on the existing housing stock where a lot of the current people live?[123]

New housing may be too expensive for the incumbent residents, but it reduces the chances that new residents will outbid low-income households for the existing housing.

The second argument is that higher property values increase property taxes, and often very rapidly and steeply. For property owners on a fixed income or with low income, the property taxes soon become a burden. Facing the threat of foreclosure by taxing authorities, many sell their properties and are displaced. But developers are not the culprits here; taxing authorities are. We will examine solutions to this problem in Chapter 19.

The third argument against gentrification is that it changes a neighborhood's character. The new residents seldom share the cultural mores of the incumbent residents. Businesses seeking to cater to the new residents open up. The result is a gradual, but steady shift in the culture of the neighborhood. When the incumbent residents no longer recognize the neighborhood, many relocate. This is called cultural displacement.

The arguments against gentrification all center on displacement. Like gentrification, displacement means different things to different people.

Economic Displacement

Anti-gentrification activists regard displacement as inherently bad. However, displacement means to move something from its current place or position to a new place or position. Displacement is a value neutral concept. In regard to housing, it means moving to a different home. Often, displacement is a voluntary, such as when someone chooses to move to a different neighborhood or apartment building. Other times, displacement occurs reluctantly. Opponents of gentrification focus on this reluctant relocation.

One example of reluctant displacement is when rents for existing housing increase. While this certainly occurs, as we saw above, it is not as severe and widespread as housing activists would like us to believe.

The story of Terry Herlihy illustrates an example of an economic cause for displacement that can occur after gentrification begins. In 1978, he bought a three-unit building in Chicago's Wicker Park neighborhood for $29,000. He lived in one unit and rented the other two. He had a nice arrangement and thought he would remain in the house the rest of his life.

However, as the neighborhood gentrified, property values appreciated. By the early 2020s, Herlihy's tax bill was more than $21,000—nearly 75 percent of what he paid for the house. Living on a fixed income, Herlihy can no longer afford the home where he has lived for more than four decades. "I'll have to sell in two years," he said in early 2021.[124]

Another long-time homeowner in Wicker Park, Carlos Flores has watched his property tax bill increase 200 percent over the past twenty years. He had to refinance his home in 2019 simply to pay his taxes and continue living there.

Because of the rising property taxes, both Herlihy and

Flores have had to increase the rents on the units they rent. Wicker Park was once an affordable area for immigrants, minorities, and working-class Chicagoans. Herlihy and Flores have not increased rents because they are greedy landlords; the increases are necessary to pay an insatiable government. Another property owner in Wicker Park has been leasing one of her units for below-market rates to the same tenant for twenty years, but increased property taxes make that more challenging. "When I bought my building," she said, "I made a commitment to keep my rents affordable to rent to families. I want to be able to give him a huge break, but that's becoming increasingly difficult. As property taxes rise, it's difficult to maintain a multi-generational building."[125]

The developers and investors who gentrify a neighborhood are often vilified for the increases in property values. Interestingly, defenders of single-family zoning argue that allowing multi-family housing will lower property values. Both the opponents of gentrification and the defenders of single-family zoning want government to intervene to prevent changes in property values.

One of the "tools" used by activists and government officials to reduce economic displacement is inclusionary zoning (IZ). Because new construction or major rehabilitation projects require permits, local governments can use the permitting process as a weapon against developers. Under IZ, developers must set aside a certain number of housing units for low-income families at below-market rates in exchange for permission to proceed with their project. The subsidized rents allow many renters to stay in the neighborhood and enjoy the benefits of gentrification, while other tenants pay for the subsidies through higher rents.

Inclusionary zoning is the flip side of exclusionary zoning (EZ). Where EZ is used to keep certain kinds of people out of a neighborhood, IZ is used to keep certain kinds of people in a neighborhood. Both are used to impose the community's values upon others. Both are a result of the Progressive framework.

Activists cite both economic and cultural reasons for supporting inclusionary zoning.

Cultural Displacement

As new residents and businesses move into a neighborhood, the area's culture often begins to change. The new businesses cater to the needs and desires of the new residents. The new residents look and act differently. While many long-time residents don't like the changes, some welcome them—at least partially. Some residents desire the new health care clinics, childcare facilities, retail shops, and restaurants that gentrification can bring. But that desire is tempered by the loss of the neighborhood's culture as the area becomes more integrated. Interestingly, some housing advocates call for more racially and economically integrated neighborhoods while opponents of gentrification often call for less racial and economic integration.

To combat cultural displacement, many community groups are demanding a Community Benefits Agreement (CBA) with developers. In some cities, such agreements are negotiated between the private parties—the community group and the developer—but in many cities the municipal government is directly involved. And if a developer doesn't satisfy the demands of the community group, the government will not grant permission to build the project. If the developer is not subservient to the demands of the collective, he will be denied permission to proceed with his project.

A CBA can include nearly anything. Most include some provision for retaining or increasing the number of below-market housing units in the area. Other agreements are much more nuanced. For example, when Rice University built a technology center in Houston's Third Ward, residents were concerned about gentrification changing the area's culture. Indeed, a 2019 study by the Baker Institute at Rice University found that a majority of residents of Houston's Third Ward were "'extremely concerned' about a loss of African-American culture in the neighborhood because of gentrification.[126] The residents formed a community organization to negotiate with Rice. The group demanded that the university repair and maintain historic sites in the neighborhood, as well as sponsor Juneteenth and Kwanzaa celebrations.

And, while many cities are rejecting exclusionary zoning by relaxing single-family zoning laws, at least one city has considered using exclusionary zoning to combat gentrification. In early 2021, Louisville Councilman Jecorey Arthur introduced a bill that would designate "historically black neighborhoods as protected zones from gentrification."[127] In other words, black neighborhoods should stay black, and Arthur wants to achieve that by using government to impose barriers to non-blacks owning property in the "protected zones."

Using government force to prevent blacks from living in certain neighborhoods because of skin color was racist and evil. Using government force to keep whites from living in certain neighborhoods because of skin color is equally racist and evil. Using government force to prevent individuals from living where they choose is an injustice. It subordinates individuals to the collective.

Change Is Not Always Pleasant

Much of the discussion regarding gentrification begins with a bias against it. Activists see change occurring and look only at the negatives, such as displacement. They fail to consider any of the positives that result from gentrification, such as better housing and more economic activity. They fail to consider the full context.

Change is not always pleasant. We can empathize with those are displaced by gentrification. But we must also recognize the benefits that result from investment in impoverished neighborhoods. Incumbent residents can enjoy and take advantage of those benefits, but only if they act to earn it.

The changes that occur in a gentrifying neighborhood are

the aggregate of hundreds or perhaps thousands of individual choices. Each of those choices is motivated by the desire to improve one's life. If the incumbent residents want to improve their lives, then they need to take the actions necessary to earn it.

The proposals to stop or slow gentrification place the group—incumbent residents—as the standard. The harm or benefit to those residents is the only concern. If we truly want to help those impacted negatively by gentrification, then we must reject the group as the standard. Instead, we must enable individuals to pursue and attain the values they desire.

THE FRAMEWORK OF THE PRESENT

Each of the contemporary proposals that we have examine have used one group or another as the standard by which to evaluate that policy. These policies have been analyzed through the lens of the benefits to the favored group.

As we saw in Part 2, each of these policies is founded on the same Progressive framework. Beginning with the group as the standard, each policy is considered in isolation—out of context. In each instance, alternatives are dismissed or not given serious consideration. Present policy proposals may differ in details from past policies, but they are aligned in their essential nature.

Ending single-family zoning is presented as a way to benefit the collective—low-income households and "people of color." Tenant protections, it is claimed, are necessary to protect the rights of the group—tenants. Advocates of rent control argue that it prevents large rent increases from impacting the same group. Housing subsidies are used to help the collective—low-income households. Efforts to stop gentrification are designed to benefit the group—the community.

From the perspective of the favored group, many of these policies will be effective in the short-term. Tenant protections do reduce evictions. Rent control does provide some renters with below-market rate housing. Housing subsidies do help the recipients obtain better housing. But while these policies are benefitting one group, they are also inflicting harm upon others. As an example, tenant protections and rent control prevent landlords from using their property as they choose, from trading on terms and conditions that they find acceptable

In focusing on the group, each of these policies is evaluated in isolation—how it will affect the preferred group. The policy is evaluated by looking only at the immediate and easily seen consequences, while the long-term and less easily seen are ignored and evaded.

If we want to end the housing crisis, then we must reject the framework that caused it. We must embrace a framework that begins with the proper standard, considers the full context, and identifies the pros and cons of alternatives. We must reject the collectivism of the Progressive framework and embrace the individualism of the framework for the future.

PART 4

The Future

Intellectual freedom cannot exist without political freedom; political freedom cannot exist without economic freedom; a free mind and a free market are corollaries. Ayn Rand

Insanity, it is often said, is doing the same thing over and over while expecting different results. Yet, for more than a century, policy makers and legislators have been following the same flawed framework regarding housing and related policies. This framework created the affordable housing crisis and its continued application has made the problem worse. Still, housing advocates and legislators cling to the Progressive framework while promising different results. It is the epitome of insanity.

We won't solve the affordable housing crisis by following the same framework that caused it. We must abandon the collectivist framework. In its place, we must embrace a new way of thinking about housing policy.

In Part 4 we will examine the individualistic framework that can solve the housing problem. We will look at alternatives to the failed policies of the past and present. If we reject those policies, and the framework upon which they are founded, we can have bright future.

Unlike the promises made by collectivists, the promises made by the individualist framework are attainable. For a century, the collectivist framework has promised safe, decent, and affordable housing for all. That promise remains unfulfilled. The individualist framework promises freedom, the freedom to rise as high as one's talents and ambitions will carry him. Individualism promises the freedom to attain the housing that one earns. Individualism does not promise or guarantee desirable results. It promises the freedom to pursue and earn desirable results.

The past is filled with broken promises and misery. The future doesn't need to be that way. But to avoid more insanity, we need a new framework.

MARKET FAILURE OR POLICY FAILURE?

Housing advocates routinely argue that the private market has failed to provide an adequate supply of affordable housing for low- and moderate-income households. If, as they claim, the market has failed, then private sector alternatives to deal with the housing shortage simply won't work.

There is truth in the claim that the private sector has not produced a sufficient supply of affordable housing. If we want to solve the housing crisis, then we must identify why this is the case. And the reason is, as we have seen, it simply isn't profitable to build housing for low- and moderate-income households. It isn't profitable because of the costs and restrictions imposed by government regulations—zoning and environmental regulations top the list.

The market hasn't failed. The market hasn't been allowed to operate because of government policies dating back more than a century.

If we want to make the best decisions regarding the housing crisis, then we must be willing to examine the pros and cons of the alternatives. And we must be clear about what the true alternatives are. If we casually dismiss some alternatives, we may not be implementing the best policies. If we do not objectively consider alternatives, we may make the problem worse.

Market Failure

Market failure is generally defined as "an inefficient distribution of goods and services in the free market. In market failure, the individual incentives for rational behavior do not lead to rational outcomes for the group."[128] Note that this definition uses the group as the standard of value.

Most of the time, supply and demand will influence prices and production. When supply is low relative to the demand, prices will rise and additional production will be incentivized. When supply is high relative to the demand, prices will decrease and production will be reduced. However, this isn't happening with low- and moderate-income housing. The demand is high relative to the supply, but production is not being increased to balance supply and demand. This, housing advocates claim, is evidence of market failure.

Rather than identify why the market isn't producing an adequate supply of housing, activists indict the market and fail to examine why this "failure" is occurring. As we have seen, government policies are a primary cause of the high cost to build new housing. If land-use regulations, environmental regulations and other government controls add more than 40 percent to the cost of new housing, it is impossible to profitably build low-income housing. In housing and many other issues, when government creates a problem, the private market takes the blame. Housing activists argue that private sector builders and developers are not building enough housing while calling for policies that will impose more controls and restrictions on those builders and developers.

Progressive activist Ian Stephens acknowledges that it is increasingly difficult to profitably build affordable housing. He goes on to say that single-family zoning restricts the availability of affordable housing. Using Berkeley as an example, he correctly states that if the land were rezoned to allow greater housing density, "Berkeley could increase effective land supply in the city and make affordable housing much more practical. If more units are allowed on a plot of land, developers are much more likely to develop because they will be able to make a profit more easily."[129]

But rezoning, he argues, will not be incentive enough for developers to build the quantity of affordable housing that the nation needs. "The only way to ensure that affordable housing is built despite these economic forces is for our government to step in to offset them." Government, he argues, must be involved by offering subsidies and tax incentives for high-density and affordable housing. Doing so will make affordable housing profitable to build. In truth, the most effective way to make low- and moderate-income housing profitable is to remove the controls and restrictions that drive up the cost.

Tax credits and subsidies are limited, and a small number of projects qualify each year. The very nature of tax incentives and subsidies limits how many housing units can be profitably built under those programs. However, in a truly free market, such limits do not exist. In a truly free market, every builder and developer could profitably build low- and moderate-income housing.

Removing controls and restrictions on housing producers is not going to immediately solve the housing crisis. It takes months, and sometimes years, for a housing project to be built. This is true with or without tax credits and subsidies. There is no quick fix. However, removing controls and restrictions will enable tens of thousands of housing producers, not just the handful who are able to secure tax credits, to profitably build affordable housing. While some housing activists agree that rezoning should be a part of the solution, others oppose the idea.

In a piece titled "When Affordable Housing Meets Free-market Fantasy," Zelda Bronstein writes, "Because affordable housing doesn't yield acceptable profits to real estate investors, the only way a substantial amount of it is going to get built is if it's publicly funded."[130] Unlike Stephens, Bronstein doesn't even attempt to identify why affordable housing doesn't yield acceptable profits. She accepts that fact as immutable, rather than the result of flawed policies.

Eliminating zoning, she argues, is "an aggressive, market-oriented, democracy-adverse approach to land use." Bronstein wants land use determined by a democratic process, yet ignores the costs imposed by exclusionary zoning and similar regulations that have been imposed by a democratic process. To address the crisis, she wants the government to spend increasing amounts of money, rather than advocate a policy that costs nothing—repealing land-use regulations.

Journalist Patrick Range McDonald dismisses the argument that the housing shortage is merely a supply and demand issue.[131] Those who make that claim, he argues, are advocating a "trickle-down policy" for the benefit of corporations and the wealthy. Like Bronstein, he argues that ending exclusionary zoning will invite "predatory developers into middle- and working-class communities, especially those of color, where land may be less expensive." He concludes that government needs to pursue policies to preserve, protect, and produce affordable housing.

These three activists represent the predominant views of housing activists regarding the free market. The market has failed, they claim, and the solution is more controls and restrictions on the market. Ignoring the fact that a century of government intervention in the housing market has made the housing crisis much worse, they call for more government intervention. They believe that only government can solve the problem that it created. The government's only tool is a hammer, and the Progressive framework sees every problem as a nail.

What McDonald calls a "trickle-down policy" is a phenomenon known as "filtering." Filtering has occurred throughout American history. Homes that were built for middle-class or upper-class individuals gradually became more affordable to lower income individuals. When an individual with a higher income moves to a more modern home, his former residence often becomes available for individuals with a lower income. And the process repeats as individuals move to better housing, thereby freeing housing for lower-income individuals.

A study by Evan Mast for the W.E. Upjohn Institute for Employment Research confirms this. He found that "new construction reduces demand and loosens the housing market in low- and middle-income areas, even in the short run."[132] Mast looked at "migration patterns" of 52,000 residents of 686 new, large multi-family buildings in central cities. He tracked them to their former apartment and then identified the new occupants. He repeated this for six rounds.

While there were factors that Mast could not quantify, he determined that 100 new market-rate units created 70 units for below-median income households, and 39 units in bottom-quintile income areas. Using a more conservative approach, he found 45 and 17 units created. Using either approach, it is clear that each new unit built increases the supply of housing for low- and moderate-income individuals.

We see this process at work with automobiles. A new luxury automobile is unaffordable to a low- or moderate-income family. However, as that vehicle ages, what was once unaffordable becomes more affordable for them.

Fundamentally, the housing crisis is an issue of supply. The supply of affordable housing for low- and moderate-income households is significantly lower than the demand. Increasing the supply of housing at any price level increases the supply of housing for families at every income level. But government policies make increasing the supply of housing more and more expensive.

While these three writers disagree about ending exclusionary zoning, they are in agreement that government must be more involved in housing. They don't want to free housing producers. They want government to use a combination of incentives and compulsion—tax credits and regulations. But these are the same policies that have failed for one-hundred years. The market hasn't been allowed to operate freely. Rather than acknowledge this fact, these advocates argue that the market has failed and want to further strangle the market.

The Housing Shortage Is A Policy Failure

The profit motive is the only incentive that builders and developers need. When producers are free of arbitrary restrictions and regulations, profit is their reward for producing the values we want and need. Developers can't make a profit producing affordable housing because they aren't free. Rather than call for more freedom for housing producers, housing activists demand policies that place more controls and restrictions on builders and developers.

The housing crisis isn't a failure of the free market. It is a failure of the interventionist housing policies of the last century. Each intervention has made the problem worse and created new problems. Time after time the "solution" has been more interventions. This is the result of clinging to the Progressive framework.

America has not had a free market in housing for more than a century. Our current system is a mixture of freedom and controls. To blame the free market for the housing shortage is disingenuous and intellectually dishonest.

For more than a century, local governments have used land-use regulations to control what housing can be built and where it can be built. The federal government has long sought to encourage home ownership through mortgage subsidies and the construction of more low-income housing through a variety of subsidies. Road policies have led to the proliferation of suburbs through subsidies to motorists. The dominant force in the nation's housing for the past century has been government policy.

Today, we hear growing calls to expand government's role in housing. We need more public housing. We need to provide financial assistance to help minorities to purchase a home. We must give subsidies to low-income renters. We must subsidize the construction of low-income housing. We must place more restrictions on landlords. These are the same policies that have been tried for more than one-hundred years, and they have failed time after time. The affordable housing shortage has not been resolved, and it has only grown worse as these policies are continued. It is insane to think that the same framework will yield different results.

Politicians believe that the same policies that created the problem will somehow solve the problem. But the same cause will always have the same effect. Changing the details of a destructive policy does not remove its destructiveness. It simply changes the amount of money spent and the number of victims.

All of these failed policies are an attempt to provide benefits to one group or another. We are told that these policies will promote the "public interest." Yet, these policies have created harm and misery for many of the individuals who comprise the public. Each of these policies disables someone, whether builders and developers, landlords, property owners, or taxpayers.

We will not solve the housing crisis if we continue with the same flawed Progressive framework. We must reject that framework. We must seriously and objectively consider alternatives policies. But to do that, we need a new framework for housing.

A New Framework For Housing

If we truly want to make the best decisions regarding housing policy, then we must be willing to consider alternatives that may not comport with our current views. If we cling to a policy even when it does not produce desirable results, then we are doing all Americans a great injustice. If we truly want to solve the housing crisis, then we must be willing to consider the possibility that government policies have not solved the problem, but instead, have made it worse. To refuse to consider such a view is to intentionally blind oneself.

A new framework for housing begins with a clearly stated goal. Housing advocates begin with the goal of providing safe, decent, affordable housing for all Americans. But this is an improper goal. It is founded on the premise that a large number of Americans are incapable of providing for their own sustenance. And so, the advocates promote interventionist policies that make production more difficult, and paternalistic policies that treat adults like children.

The proper goal is to enable individuals—all individuals—to earn the housing that they desire. This goal is founded on the premise that individuals can make rational choices and provide for their own well-being. But to do that, individuals must be free to act as they think best. Freedom enables each individual to pursue his dreams in every aspect of life, including housing. Interventionist policies disable some for the alleged benefit of others. The individualistic framework enables everyone and disable no one.

The second leg of a new framework is identifying and considering the full context. Housing advocates look at issues in isolation, refusing to consider other relevant issues. They begin with a conclusion and then seek facts that support that conclusion while ignoring contradictory facts. Only by beginning with the proper goal and a consideration of the full context will we be able to identify the best policy.

Considering the full context means examining related and relevant issues and identifying their interrelationship. It means identifying how a policy will impact other issues, not just today, but far into the future. It means looking past the easily seen and searching for the unseen. Only when we consider the full context can we choose the best policy to accomplish our goal. Considering the full context is neither easy nor automatic. It takes effort and thought, often over a period of time.

The final step of the new framework is to consider the pros and cons of alternatives. Housing advocates are quick to dismiss private sector alternatives without bothering to examine benefits that might be attained. They fail to consider the negative consequences of increased government intervention in housing and speak only of the alleged benefits. By looking at only the cons of private sector alternatives and only the pros of government intervention, housing advocates blind themselves to solutions that might actually solve the housing crisis, rather than make it worse.

Examining the pros and cons of alternatives requires an honest evaluation of the facts, and not just the facts that are easily obtained or supportive of our position. We must be willing to step outside of our "echo chamber" and consider conflicting viewpoints. In evaluating alternatives, we must consider all of the relevant facts, only the relevant facts, and nothing but the relevant facts.

So far, we have examined government policies relating to housing for the past one-hundred years. We have also examined contemporary policies regarding housing. We have looked at the full context, including issues that are not obviously related to housing, such as road policies, minimum wage laws, and occupational licensing. We will now turn our attention to alternatives to the policies of the past and the present. These alternatives are founded on a new framework for housing policy decision making. These alternatives enable all individuals, not by disabling others, but by protecting each individual's right to pursue his values.

ALTERNATIVES TO ZONING

Defenders of exclusionary zoning argue that if that institution is eliminated, neighborhoods will be overrun with multi-family housing. Quiet neighborhoods where children can play in the front yard will be transformed with increased traffic, denser housing, and a myriad of other ills. Zoning, they claim, is necessary to have the kind of neighborhood that they desire.

It is understandable that individuals may not want to live near apartment buildings, condominiums, and other multi-family housing. But this can be accomplished without the coercive measures that are zoning. We can enable everyone to earn the housing they desire without resorting to coercive, disabling policies. Non-coercive means can be used to create and protect neighborhoods. Indeed, these means are used throughout the country today. But first, let us look at a city that has never had zoning.

Houston: A City Without Zoning

In 1990, city officials in Houston proposed a zoning ordinance for the city and began drawing zoning maps. Zoning advocates made many claims about zoning. It would protect neighborhoods and empower the people. It would be built on a consensus and promote economic growth. Without zoning, developers would overbuild, and the city would be overrun with vacant strip centers. Industry would relocate to the middle of residential neighborhoods. For nearly three years, Houstonians debated zoning. In November 1993, voters rejected zoning for the third time. Today, Houston is the only major American city without zoning.

The dire predictions made by zoning advocates have not materialized in the thirty years since zoning was last proposed. Houston is not a ghost town filled with vacant buildings and weed infested lots. For decades, the city has had one of the nation's most robust economies. Its population has grown by nearly 40 percent since zoning was proposed in 1990. Of the nation's ten largest cities, Houston had the second most affordable single-family housing in the second quarter of 2022.[133] In short, Houston demonstrates that a city can thrive without coercive zoning laws.

Without zoning, builders and developers can change land uses without enduring the delays and expenses inherent in zoning. As more Houstonians want to live closer to downtown, areas that were once economically depressed and filled with vacant lots and dilapidated housing, now have a variety of housing options and are bustling with restaurants and retail shops. In Houston, developers can quickly respond to changing consumer demands without first groveling at the feet of government bureaucrats for permission to do so. Those builders and developers are the ones truly serving the public.

Mixed-use neighborhoods are common inside the city's inner beltway. For example, The Heights—a neighborhood near downtown—contains upgraded Victorian-style homes, garden apartments, modern mid-rises, office buildings, restaurants, and a variety of commercial businesses. These all exist in close proximity to one another without problems. This phenomenon is present throughout the city's inner loop.

There are also a considerable number of neighborhoods that are exclusively single-family homes. Residential neighborhoods have not been overrun with multi-family housing, industry, or commercial establishments.

In Houston, developers can build the type of housing that consumers want, and that housing can be built where

Houstonians want to live. In cities with zoning, developers can only build what government officials will approve, and they can build only where officials allow it. The absence of zoning allows Houston's developers to offer consumers a wide range of housing options.

The absence of zoning has not led to the evils predicted by zoning's defenders. That is because there are non-coercive means to address undesirable land uses.

Nuisance Laws

Nuisance has its roots in common law, and it holds that a property owner has the right to the peaceful use of his property. A neighbor who blasts loud music at midnight or sends noxious smoke into your yard is preventing you from peacefully using your property. But loud music and noxious smoke are not, in and of themselves, a nuisance. Context matters.

An action may constitute a nuisance in one context but not another. For example, if you use a grill in your back yard, you will likely generate some smoke. But the amount of smoke is unlikely to impact your neighbors. However, if you built a giant bonfire in your backyard and sent plumes of smoke into your neighbors' yards, you have created a nuisance. That same bonfire in the middle of 1,000 acre ranch will not negatively impact anyone.

In each of these examples, the same action occurs— generating smoke. But in two instances, the smoke does not prevent others from using their property and is not a nuisance. Nuisance laws enable individuals to use their property as they choose, so long as they respect the freedom of others to use their property as they choose.

In contrast, zoning prohibits certain types of land use regardless of the context. Indeed, zoning was first presented as a way to eliminate nuisances while ignoring the contextual nature of nuisance. Zoning became a blanket condemnation of certain types of land uses. Commercial activities, for example, are prohibited by single-family zoning, even though such uses are often unobtrusive and even welcomed by nearby residents. Many homeowners would welcome a veterinary clinic, dentist, or mechanic within walking distance. Exclusionary zoning makes this impossible by disabling property owners.

To illustrate the potential benefits of commercial activities near neighborhoods, my mechanic has a shop less than one-hundred yards from my front door. They open at 8AM and close at 5PM, so they are not disturbing nearby homeowners at night. For me, the location is very convenient. I can drop off my truck in the morning, walk home, and then walk to get it later in the day. The entire trip takes less than ten minutes in total walking time. Unlike when I take my truck to the dealership, I don't have to wait for hours or get a ride from and back to the shop.

Commercial activities per se do not create a nuisance or violate anyone's rights. Short-term rentals (STRs), such as Airbnb, are an example. Many homeowners object to STRs, claiming that they are nothing but "party houses." They want to ban or severely restrict STRs, often via zoning laws.

If the tenants of an STR play loud music late at night, throw trash around the neighborhood, or otherwise disrupt neighbors' right to the peaceful use of their property, then a nuisance has been created and the tenants should be prosecuted. If an STR owner repeatedly allows his property to serve as a party house, then he too should be prosecuted. However, if the tenants are quiet and are respectful of the neighbors, there is no nuisance and no rights have been violated.

Unlike zoning, nuisance laws respect property rights. Unlike zoning, nuisance laws are non-coercive. They recognize a property owner's right to use his land as he chooses, so long as he doesn't disturb others. And when property owners are free, they can and will find innovative ways to use their land without infringing on the rights of others, even when that use might be deemed "incompatible."

When the demand for housing in a neighborhood

increases, but the supply is artificially restricted by zoning, prices will rise. But if the supply can keep pace with the demand, prices will moderate. Freed of the arbitrary restrictions imposed by zoning, housing producers will find innovative ways to build unobtrusive housing and commercial establishments where people want to live, work, and play. Unlike zoning, nuisance laws respect the property owner's freedom to use his land as he chooses, so long as he respects the freedom of others to do the same.

Nuisance laws don't prevent individuals from playing loud music, generating obnoxious smoke, or throwing trash around a neighborhood. Neither does zoning. However, nuisance laws do provide an objective way to prosecute those who do not respect the rights of others. Zoning is pre-emptive—stopping certain land uses even when no rights have been violated. Nuisance is curative—it applies only when rights have been violated.

There will be some who don't want to live near any form of multi-family housing or commercial activity. They want to live in a single-family neighborhood. Deed restrictions are a non-coercive way to achieve this.

Deed Restrictions

Deed restrictions, sometimes called covenants, are a contractual agreement between property owners to limit how they use their land. Deed restrictions are widely used around the country and are often put in place by a developer when a neighborhood is first developed. Deed restrictions typically create a homeowners' association (HOA) to enforce the agreement.

Deed restrictions can prohibit or require nearly any detail of the property's use. They might prohibit commercial activities, require a home of a minimum size, allow a limited number of exterior paint colors, or a myriad of other details. They might mandate single-family homes, or allow accessory dwelling units, duplexes, or other types of housing.

While the provisions of deed restrictions often appear similar to those of zoning, there is a crucial difference. Zoning is coercive and mandatory. Deed restrictions are contractual and voluntary. Zoning applies to an entire city. Deed restrictions only apply to a specific neighborhood. If an individual doesn't like the restrictions in one neighborhood, he can move to a neighborhood with restrictions more to his liking, or no restrictions at all. Certainly, if he doesn't like the provisions of a municipality's zoning laws, he can move to another city. But this might mean that he must live far from his job, family, or the area where he wants to live.

Most deed restrictions include provisions for amending or changing the restrictions. These usually require a vote of property owners. Zoning also allows for amendments and changes, but these must be approved by zoning officials. When zoning changes are proposed, public hearings are held, and non-property owners are allowed to voice their objections to how the actual owners want to use their property. Deed restrictions limit the discussion of changes to those who own property in the neighborhood; zoning invites anyone with an agenda to make demands.

As mentioned above, deed restrictions are typically put in place by the developer. However, if single-family zoning were eliminated and a neighborhood has no deed restrictions, property owners could still use deed restrictions to create or maintain the type of neighborhood they want.

Because deed restrictions are voluntary, property owners can unilaterally place restrictions on their own land. Without zoning, each owner would be free to choose whether to place restrictions on his property, as well as what types of restrictions. A neighborhood could develop a standard set of restrictions and allow each property owner to accept, reject, or modify those restrictions as the owner thinks best for him.

It is unlikely that all property owners will elect to place restrictions on their land, but this doesn't detract from the usefulness of deed restrictions in the absence of zoning. For example, if half of the property owners in a neighborhood agreed to restrict their land to single-family homes, it would be much more difficult for a developer to assemble a parcel large enough for a big apartment complex.

But let us assume a "worse-case" scenario in which no property owners choose to impose restrictions on their land. If this occurred, then it is obvious that they aren't concerned about changing land uses. Each property owner would be free to act on his own evaluation of the situation. The property owners, not a noisy gang of agitators, would have control. Deed restrictions enable property owners to control how their land is used while zoning disables that control.

For neighborhoods that don't currently have deed restrictions, eliminating zoning will pose certain challenges. Absent deed restrictions, developers could buy large parcels of land and rapidly change the neighborhood. But property owners would have choices. They could place restrictions on their land. They could refuse to sell to the developer. They could sell and reap the rewards. Zoning eliminates such choices. Deed restrictions are the individualistic solution to undesirable land uses. Zoning is the collectivist solution.

The New Framework

Zoning is based on the premise that government should control and dictate land use, regardless of the owner's desires or values. There is no justice in such centralized planning, for it negates and destroys the planning of individuals, not because they have violated the rights of others, but because they want to do something that bureaucrats don't approve of. Those who act contrary to the dictates of zoning officials are subject to fines, jail, or both.

In contrast to the coercive nature of zoning, nuisance and deed restrictions respect property rights. Both enable property owners to make choices and act accordingly, while respecting the rights of others to do the same. Houston provides an enlightening example of this.

If we want to enable individuals to pursue the values that are important to them, then we must enable them to act on their choices, so long as they respect the freedom of others to do the same. If we want housing justice, then we must enable individuals and families to earn the housing that they desire. That means eliminating disabling laws like zoning and land-use regulations and embracing the individualistic framework.

HOUSING ALTERNATIVES

In many American cities, as much as 75 percent of the land is zoned for single-family homes. Such restrictions severely limit the housing that can legally be built in a city, and this is a primary cause of the nation's housing shortage.

In addition to restricting land use to single-family homes, exclusionary zoning generally prohibits alternative forms of housing, such as mobile homes and modular homes. This too contributes to the rising cost of housing. Site-built homes are labor intensive, and automation is virtually impossible. As a result, site-built homes are considerably more expensive than manufactured housing.

As we saw in the last chapter, eliminating single-family zoning does not mean that neighborhoods would be transformed into a sea of apartment buildings. Nor does it mean that neighborhoods would become giant mobile home parks. Deed restrictions can be used to prohibit certain land uses, including mobile and modular housing. But unlike zoning, the choice is for each property owner to make. Without zoning, property owners will be free to produce alternative housing and increase the supply of affordable housing.

Legalizing "Middle" Housing

Defenders of single-family zoning present a false alternative. If a neighborhood isn't restricted to single-family homes, they claim, the alternative is large apartment buildings. Such claims ignore a significant number of alternatives—so-called "middle" housing.

As the name implies, middle housing falls between single-family homes and large apartment buildings. Middle housing consists of such alternatives as duplexes, cottages, small apartment buildings (six units or less), and rooming houses. Such housing alternatives were common in many American neighborhoods prior to zoning. Zoning made them illegal in neighborhoods across the nation, giving birth to the housing crisis.

There is nothing inherently offensive about middle housing. When designed well, middle housing blends with the neighborhood and complements the other buildings. Even if a building is poorly designed, bad taste does not violate anyone's rights. A crucial aspect of freedom is accepting the fact that others may make choices that we find offensive.

Cities across the country are beginning to understand the role that zoning has played in the housing crisis. They are relaxing their zoning restrictions and allowing middle housing in neighborhoods previously limited to single family homes. Minneapolis allows up to three housing units per lot. Charlotte now permits duplexes and triplexes throughout the city. And California has passed legislation that allows up to ten units on a lot. While these measures still impose restrictions on property owners, they do allow for more freedom in land use and greater housing density. The result will be more middle housing.

In 2020, the first year that duplexes and triplexes were legal in Minneapolis, sixteen duplexes and three triplexes were built. Another twenty-two buildings were converted to a duplex or triplex. In total, seventy units were added to the housing stock.[134] Many have used these numbers to argue that seventy units is insignificant in a growing city of more than 420,000 people. Eliminating single-family, they argue, is not making much of a difference. These numbers may seem paltry compared to the numbers of people government programs promise to help, but we must remember that 2020 was a year marked by lockdowns, supply chain disrupts, and prolonged uncertainty. Indeed, by March 2021, another twenty-eight duplexes and seven triplexes had been built in Minneapolis.[135] With supply chains improving and uncertainty diminishing, in the first three months of 2021 builders and developers added more duplexes and triplexes than all of 2020.

There are two important lessons from the numbers in Minneapolis. First, eliminating exclusionary zoning does not result in a dramatic and immediate transformation of single-family neighborhoods. A few small, multi-family properties in a neighborhood is hardly disruptive to the residents. Second, when some freedom is restored to property owners, some—but certainly not all—will change land uses and add housing to the stock. It will take time for the supply to substantially increase, but government programs also take time and rarely accomplish their stated objectives. The housing crisis was not created overnight, and it won't be solved overnight. We must have reasonable expectations.

The Empire State Building in New York City provides an example of what developers can do when they are not shackled by zoning and a byzantine permitting process. Construction on the iconic building started March 17, 1930. It was completed one year and forty-five days later. Today, it can take years just to obtain the permits required to start construction. That permitting process slows construction and adds to its costs.

Eliminating single-family zoning does not have the results that zoning's defenders claim. At the same time, it will not result in the immediate construction of the number of new affordable housing units a city needs. Eliminating single-family zoning is only one part of the solution. Another part of the solution is to allow mixed-use communities.

Legalizing Mixed-Use Communities

As the name implies, a mixed-use community has a diversity of land uses, including single-family housing, multi-family housing, and commercial uses. Prior to zoning, most neighborhoods in America were mixed use.

The limitations of travel in the late nineteenth century and early twentieth century necessitated the proximity of housing and businesses. Butchers, grocers, barbers, and other businesses conveniently provided the goods and services residents needed. Today, a growing number of individuals want to live in "walkable," that is, mixed-use communities. They want to be close to restaurants, bars, retail, and work. They want the convenience that once existed in most American cities.

As with small, multi-family housing, mixed land uses are not inherently disruptive to a neighborhood. Certainly, businesses with a high traffic volume would cause disruptions, but businesses such as dentists, veterinary clinics, realtors, cafes, and florists generally do not have a large traffic volume. And the presence of such businesses provides convenience for residents.

Unfortunately, many view such mixed uses as "incompatible." They think that land uses should be segregated, as if the presence of a doctor's office or bistro down the street will somehow ruin the neighborhood.

In the last chapter we saw how nuisance laws can be used to objectively identify land uses that are truly disruptive. The fact that we find something offensive does not mean that it is infringing on our rights. It is worth remembering that during much of the twentieth century, many Americans believed that people of different races and ethnicities were "incompatible." Today, we recognize the injustice in that view. It is time that we recognize the injustice of declaring certain land uses "incompatible."

Further, we also saw how deed restrictions can be used to voluntarily keep businesses out of a neighborhood. A neighborhood that does not want commercial activities within its border has a non-coercive way to achieve that goal.

Virtually every housing policy of the past century has been founded on government coercion. Whether it was the use of zoning for economic and racial segregation, taking money from taxpayers to build roads and subsidize suburban living, destroying neighborhoods for "urban renewal," or placing prohibitions and mandates on landlords for the purpose of protecting "tenants' rights," housing policies are dominated by coercion. Those policies have only made the situation worse because they are inherently disabling.

If we truly want to solve the housing crisis, then we must restore freedom to housing producers and property owners. We must respect their moral right to use their property as they choose. We must enable them to produce the housing that our nation so desperately needs. Doing so will unleash the innovative potential of every property owner in America. For a century, Americans have relied on government for solutions to housing problems. The collectivist framework hasn't solved the housing crisis, and it has made the problem worse. The individualistic framework enables every property owner to contribute to the solution if he so desires.

Government is an agency of force. For more than a century, that force has been used to restrict, control, and regulate the production of housing. In the process, factions and pressure groups compete to influence legislators to pass more restrictions, controls, and regulations on the producers. A growing number of Americans are rejecting one policy —exclusionary zoning—that is founded on the Progressive framework. If we truly want to solve the housing crisis, we must reject all policies founded on that framework.

Manufactured Housing

As noted previously, many zoning laws prohibit manufactured housing in residential areas. Site-built homes require extensive labor and virtually no aspect of the construction process can be automated. This contributes to the high cost of housing and lack of profit in building low- and moderate-income housing.

Manufactured housing—mobile homes, modular homes,

and similar alternatives—can be built in factories and this enables much of the process to be automated. Automation increases productivity and lowers costs, thereby enabling housing to be offered for a lower price. Further, construction is not weather dependent and can occur twenty-four hours a day, every day of the year.

While manufactured housing has long had a poor reputation, the quality has improved significantly over the past few decades. Today's manufactured housing often has the same quality and features as a site-built home. Illustrating the diverse solutions that innovators can find, factory-built housing includes mobile homes, modular homes, and shipping container homes.

Mobile homes are the most familiar form of manufactured housing. Mobile homes are built on a chassis. When wheels are attached to the chassis, the home can be towed to a location for installation. Most mobile homes come in two categories—single-wide are 14'-18' x 66'-80'), and double-wide (at least 20' wide and no more than 90' long). Larger custom units can also be manufactured.

In my early twenties, I owned a double-wide mobile home. It had three bedrooms, two bathrooms, a laundry room, kitchen, dining room, and living room and was more spacious than any apartment I have ever had. Most importantly, it provided me with decent, affordable housing in a location where I wanted to live.

The construction of modular homes is similar to mobile homes, except the home is not mounted to a chassis. Instead of being towed to the home site, it is delivered by truck and then placed in position with a crane. Each module consists of walls, ceiling, flooring, wiring and plumbing. The modules can be mixed and matched, allowing the buyer to easily customize the home. The modules can even be stacked, allowing for multi-story housing.

Boxabl illustrates the types of innovations that are possible. The company builds modular homes with a twist, or more accurately, a hinge. Each module folds into a box about the size of a shipping container. This allows the home to be transported without the wide-load permits and other expenses required for moving other types of manufactured housing. Company founder Galiano Tiramani said,

> We've got a new way to build housing that's better, cheaper, faster and can help solve the worldwide housing crisis. The goal of Boxabl is to dramatically reduce housing costs by making building construction compatible with assembly line mass production. We see a huge opportunity to transition the world from building by hand, to using the same factory principles that we use for all our other modern products.[136]

The company's first product was a 20' by 20' studio. It came with a full kitchen, bathroom, laundry area, and living room/bedroom. The Casita sold for less than $50,000. The modules can be stacked or placed side-by-side to create an unlimited number of floor plans.

Another innovation is the shipping container home offered by several companies. These homes are refurbished shipping containers and are similar to modular homes. Like other forms of modular homes, shipping container homes can be stacked or placed side-by-side in an almost unlimited number of configurations.

According to the Manufactured Housing Institute, nearly 95,000 manufactured homes were produced in 2020. This was about 10 percent of the new housing produced in the country that year. The average price was $81,900, or $57 per square foot compared to a price of $119 per square foot for a site-built home. Today, more than twenty-two million Americans live in manufactured housing.[137] While many look down their noses at manufactured housing, a significant number of Americans call them home.

A final innovation was first offered by Sears, Montgomery Ward, and other companies in the early twentieth century—a house kit. The kits came with all of the materials required to build a house. Sears was the leader in the industry, offering 370 different floor plans. The company sold more than 70,000 kits from 1908 to 1940. One of the best-selling floor plans—the Argyle—sold for $2,349 in 1923 (that is $38,181 in 2021 dollars).

Today, numerous companies, including Home Depot, offer similar kits. One kit is a 820 square foot bungalow with two bedrooms that sells for just under $40,000. The manufacturer—Imagine Kit Homes—offers more than 1,000 different home designs.

Manufactured housing represents an opportunity to greatly lower the cost of housing. But for that to occur, such housing must be legal in the places that individuals want to live.

The New Framework

The cost of site-built homes continues to climb and long ago became unaffordable for low- and moderate-income households. However, affordable housing can be built. Unfortunately, many jurisdictions prohibit manufactured housing or segregate it in designated areas. Consequently, while affordable housing options exist, government policies often make it impossible to utilize these innovations to address the housing crisis.

Eliminating single-family zoning is only one part of the solution to the housing shortage. Eliminating exclusionary zoning will allow housing producers to build the housing we need in the places people want to live. Increasing the housing stock is the only rational solution to a housing shortage. In addition to freeing housing producers, we must also free property owners. We must restore their freedom to use their land as they think best, including installing manufactured housing.

America's entrepreneurs and innovators have the ability and desire to tackle the nation's housing shortage. All they need is the freedom to do so.

ALTERNATIVES TO SUBSIDIES

If we restore freedom to housing producers, they will be enabled to build more housing. If we restore freedom to housing consumers, they will be enabled to improve their financial position and afford better housing.

However, there will be those who are unable to support themselves. The number of people who are truly incapacitated and unable to produce is smaller than we are often led to believe. Those individuals must rely on private charity and non-profits for their housing.

It is important to recognize a crucial distinction between private charity and "government charity"—i.e., subsidies. Private charity is supported through voluntary contributions. "Government charity" is supported through taxation. Private charity allows you to choose which organizations and causes to support. Subsidies remove that choice. The collectivist framework uses coercion to provide benefits to a particular group. The individualistic framework enables every individual to earn the benefits that he desires and donate as he deems appropriate.

Supporting One's Values

Private charity allows individuals to donate to the causes and organizations of their choosing. It allows individuals to support their values through non-coercive means. In contrast, "government charity" forces taxpayers to financially support programs and policies that those taxpayers may not agree with. Subsidies "enable" the recipients by disabling those who are forced to finance the subsidies.

Those who want to help low- and moderate-income households obtain better housing can donate time, money, or other resources to that cause. Those who are not concerned about such housing issues should be free to use their money for purposes of their choosing, including, their own housing.

Some housing activists may argue that the needs of low- and moderate-income households far exceeds the resources of private charities and non-profit housing producers. This may be true, but we must also remember that governments spend hundreds of billions of dollars each year on housing. If that money were not taken from taxpayers, individuals would have a substantial amount of money to donate as they thought best. Granted, many will not donate a penny to housing causes, but it is their money, and they have a moral right to choose how it is spent.

Further, the needs of low- and moderate-income households are not a claim on the property of others. Those others—those bearing the financial burden—have their own needs to satisfy. To take from them against their judgment is an injustice.

If an insufficient amount of money is raised for housing organizations and causes, then it would be clear that individuals don't think that those organizations and causes are worthwhile. If, when given the choice to donate or not, individuals choose to refrain from donating, they have made their priorities and values clear. Government programs eliminate that choice and force taxpayers to "donate" regardless of their own desires and values.

A lack of voluntary support for charity and non-profit housing does not justify using coercive measures to obtain funding. If your neighbor waved a gun in your face and demanded that you give him money to pay his rent, you would recognize his action as robbery. The principle does not change if the government acts as his proxy and takes your money to subsidize the neighbor's rent.

Mackenzie Scott provides a compelling example of supporting one's values. The former wife of Jeff Bezos, Scott donated $436 million to Habitat for Humanity and its affiliates. Of course, very few people can make a donation of the magnitude of Scott. But even small donations add up, and each individual should have the freedom to choose where his money goes.

Just as we must restore freedom of choice to the production and consumption of housing, as well as freedom of choice in how we earn a living, we must also restore freedom of choice in the realm of providing aid to the less fortunate.

Non-Profit Housing Producers

Non-profit housing organizations come in a variety of sizes, shapes, and purposes. Some are national, while others are regional or local. Some build and operate low-income housing, while others focus on helping entire communities improve housing and amenities. Currently, most non-profits are heavily dependent on funding from government agencies.

An example of a national non-profit is the Local Initiatives Support Corporation (LISC). LSIC has thirty-eight offices serving forty-five states. It pools money from government, foundations, and for-profit companies, and then provides funding, as well as technical and managerial assistance to local developers and partners who then build housing for low- and moderate-income households.

Since its start in 1979, LISC has invested more than $24 billion to develop more than 460,000 affordable homes and apartments, along with seventy-four million square feet of retail, commercial, and community space. Community space includes parks and recreational areas, schools, and farmers' markets.[138] LISC also operates more than two dozen Financial Opportunity Centers to provide job placement, financial coaching, and other resources to help individuals improve their long-term economic prospects.

Another national non-profit is Enterprise Community Partners (ECP). ECP provides investment opportunities for investors, financing for developers, advisory services, and technical assistance. During its forty-year history, ECP has invested $44 billion to develop or preserve more than 780,000 affordable housing units. To help overcome the legacy of past racist policies, ECP has pledged to invest $3.5 billion in "Black, Indigenous, and People of Color (BIPOC) and other historically marginalized housing providers to change the types of homes that get built, where they're built, who builds them and the wealth that they generate."[139] ECP is a perfect example of putting one's money where one's mouth is, i.e., financially supporting a cause that that one advocates.

Non-profits set rents below market rates to make their housing affordable for low- and moderate-income households. However, this can create cash flow problems when rents do not provide enough income for repairs and maintenance. The housing then falls into disrepair and begins to deteriorate. This is a challenge that non-profits must prepare for.

Perhaps the most widely known non-profit housing producer is Habitat for Humanity. Founded in 1976, Habitat uses volunteer labor to build homes in more than seventy countries. The organization has helped more than thirty-five million people build, preserve, or rehabilitate their home. It is the largest non-profit home builder in the world.

An innovative program offered by Habitat allows a homebuyer to help contractors and volunteers build his home. The buyer is expected to invest five-hundred hours of labor into the project, and this "sweat equity" serves as a down payment. Habitat then provides a low-interest mortgage to the buyer and payments are limited to 30 percent of the household income.

Habitat also operates other programs, such as A Brush with Kindness. This program focuses on exterior maintenance, such as painting, minor repairs, and landscaping. The Global

Village Trips program allows volunteers to travel to a foreign location of their choice and spend one to two weeks building homes. A final program, Women Build encourages women to get involved in home construction. Lowes is a major sponsor of the program, which has built more than 1,400 homes around the world.

A final category of non-profit housing provider is the community development corporation (CDC). There are an estimated four-thousand-six-hundred CDCs across the country. CDCs range from large, professionally managed organizations offering a variety of services, including affordable housing, job placement, and day care to small community groups that meet in a church basement.

One of the largest is the New Community Corporation in Newark, New Jersey, which owns and manages two-thousand units of housing and employs more than five people. New Community owns eight mid-rise buildings for seniors, handicapped, and disabled individuals, as well as a one-hundred-seventy-three-unit mid-rise and more than three-hundred townhouses and duplexes for families.

Though most CDCs are heavily dependent on government grants and donations from foundations, some are finding ways to diversify their income. As an example, the Hispanic Housing Development Corporation (HHDC) has operated throughout Chicago for more than forty years, and it has built one-thousand eight-hundred apartments and homes for families and the elderly. The HHDC also includes a for-profit construction company, the Tropic Construction Corporation, which hires and trains individuals from the communities that the organization serves.

Corporations

Businesses need employees, and employees need an affordable place to live. When affordable housing isn't available within a reasonable commute to a job, businesses have trouble attracting and retaining workers. Several companies are addressing this problem directly.

One example is Apple, which has committed $2.5 billion to help address the affordable housing shortage in California. The company will use the money to fund projects that might not otherwise be possible, as well as assist first-time home buyers. In the program's first eighteen months, thousands of families —two-thirds of which were minorities—were able to buy their first home. In addition, funds have been provided to provide financial and rental assistance to more than fifteen-thousand families impacted by the pandemic. The company also funds a non-profit project called Destination: Home, that has helped build more than one-thousand new units of deeply affordable housing and supportive housing in Silicon Valley. The company has also donated $300 million of land for affordable housing.

Similarly, Amazon has created a $2 billion Housing Equity Fund. The fund will provide grants and below-market financing for low- and moderate-income housing in Amazon's three headquarters locations: Puget Sound, Arlington, Virginia, and Nashville, Tennessee. The company's goal is to create or preserve twenty-thousand affordable homes in the three regions.

The fund's first investments included $381.9 million in loans and grants to preserve and create one-thousand-three-hundred affordable homes in Arlington and $185.5 million to preserve up to one-thousand units in King County, Washington. The company's efforts are focused on helping households making between 30 percent and 80 percent of the area's median income.

Microsoft has committed $750 million to affordable housing. Much of the company's effort is focused on middle-income households. These households often do not qualify for government subsidies and struggle to find affordable housing. The company has developed an innovative financing approach called the Middle-Income Tax-Exempt Mezzanine program that attracts private investment. The program uses bonds to provide investors with steady returns and a lowered risk for their investment.

These technology companies are putting their money where their mouth is. They are supporting causes that are important to them. All individuals should have that same freedom.

Community Land Trusts

Community land trusts (CLTs) are an innovative way to lower the cost of purchasing a home. In a CLT, ownership of land and the homes on it are separated. The trust owns the land, and an individual owns the house. As we have seen, the value of a lot can be substantial. By separating ownership, the cost of purchasing a house can be significantly reduced and become more affordable for low- and moderate-income households.

The first CLT in America was formed in 1970 on a 5,735-acre farm in Albay, Georgia. Called New Communities, the CLT was a collective farm owned by blacks. About ten families held long-term leases and dozens more worked on the farm. The farmers used roadside stands to sell the produce that they grew, built a smokehouse for curing the hogs that they raised, and installed a sugar mill to attract visitors.

In the early 1980s, a severe drought struck southeast Georgia. New Communities applied for an emergency loan from the United States Department of Agriculture (USDA). While most white farmers were granted loans, New Communities' application was denied with no explanation. Shortly thereafter, the CLT lost ownership of the land. However, following a successful lawsuit, the former landowners were awarded $12.8 million in restitution from the USDA. Two of the founders of the original New Communities quickly bought land and re-established their dream.

Today, there are about three-hundred CLTs in the United States. Many are in urban area where land values can be prohibitively high. The largest CLT in the nation is the

Champlain Housing Trust in Vermont, which owns more than $223 million of assets.

The details and operations of CLTs vary. However, nearly all CLTs share a central purpose—to produce permanently affordable housing. They do this through a combination of new construction and by rehabilitating older buildings. Some engage in other types of development, such as commercial and retail to create economic opportunities and jobs within the community.

Many CLTs are involved in other types of community improvements, such as creating parks and recreational areas. Some offer educational programs. Because the homeowners are members of the trust, they have a voice in the community's development and programs. The homeowners, not politicians and bureaucrats, make decisions about a community.

The Negative Side Of Community Land Trusts

While reducing the cost of a home purchase is a good thing, there are some negative aspects to CLTs. CLTs can be a beneficial alternative, but home buyers must be fully informed of what they are agreeing to. If they aren't fully informed, they may be in for some very rude surprises in the future. Because the goal of a CLT is to create permanently affordable housing, there are stipulations on what a particular house can be sold for in the future. Consequently, even if a home's value appreciates significantly, the owner will not realize all of the increased equity.

The Northwest Montana Community Land Trust provides an example. When a homeowner is ready to sell, the trust will purchase the home for a price that equals the original price plus 25 percent of the increase in appraised value. The trust then resells the house for the same price it paid. While home prices will increase, the amount is limited. If a household understands this, then a CLT may be a very viable alternative. However, if they don't understand this, they could receive a very shocking surprise when then sell their house. An example of this happened in New Jersey.

In 1993, Leonora Wright bought a house for $78,900 in Jersey City through a program offered by the Department of Housing and Urban Development. The program set limits on what the homes could be sold for during the next twenty years. If Wright remained in the home for more than twenty years, she could sell it for market value. Just as she was about to close on the sale of the home for $410,000, she was informed that she could keep only 5 percent of the money above the "maximum restricted sale price." That came to half of the sales price. The city would keep the rest. Wright cancelled the sale.

The program through which Wright bought her home wasn't a part of a CLT, but the restrictions were similar. Wright claims that she was not informed of the restrictions. Whether that is the case or not, it illustrates the importance of buyers being fully informed of what they are getting into. A CLT may be a good option for a household, but individuals can only make that decision if they are fully informed and can consider the full context.

The New Framework

Those who are unable to earn the housing they desire must necessarily rely on others to provide that housing. Government subsidies force taxpayers to provide financial assistance for housing, regardless of an individual taxpayer's desires, choices, or own needs.

Private charity allows those who are concerned about housing for low- and moderate-income households to put their money where their mouth. Individuals who want to help those households are free to do so, and individuals who don't want to are also free to spend their money as they desire.

If we truly want to solve the housing crisis, then we must move away from policies founded on coercion and embrace policies found on the voluntary consent of those involved. That means more freedom in land use, and more freedom in deciding how one's money is spent.

ALTERNATIVES FOR REDUCING DISPLACEMENT

One of the primary complaints about gentrification is displacement. Perhaps the predominant way this occurs is when long-time residents, whether renters or homeowners, can no longer afford to live in the neighborhood that they have long called home.

Gentrification brings investment to the neighborhood. Housing is improved. When restaurants, bars, and retail stores open in the neighborhood, residents have more choices and employment opportunities. New or improved parks, health care clinics, and other services offer amenities that were previously lacking. In short, gentrification often transforms an impoverished neighborhood in a vibrant community.

However, if long-time residents can no longer afford to live in the neighborhood, they can't enjoy the improvements being made. Displacement is an understandable concern.

Defining Displacement

Before we examine ways that displacement can be reduced, we should first be clear on what the term means and doesn't mean. One definition of displacement is "the act of forcing people or animals to leave the area where they live." Whether they explicitly accept this definition, when housing advocates address displacement, this definition is implied.

According to this definition, and indeed many housing advocates, if an individual would prefer to remain in his home but can't, he is being forced to move. For example, in a piece titled "Displacement: The misunderstood crisis," Karen Chapple writes that "displacement occurs when housing or neighborhood conditions force moves."[140] Saying that displacement is a forced move might be acceptable colloquially. However, we are discussing government policy and greater precision is required if we want to make the best choices. We must be clear what constitutes an act of force and what doesn't.

Some divide displacement into three categories. Direct displacement occurs when residents can no longer afford to live in the neighborhood. Indirect displacement occurs when low-income households move out of a housing unit, but higher rents prevent other low-income families from moving in. Cultural displacement occurs when, according to the City of Seattle, "people choose to move because their neighbors and culturally related businesses have left the area."[141] Of these three categories, cultural displacement is clearly a result of individual choices. An individual can choose to accept new neighbors and businesses, or he can choose to move. To call his choice a forced move is intellectually bankrupt. Let us take a closer look at direct and indirect displacement as they relate to rental housing.

We must remember that a lease is a contractual agreement for a specific period of time. This is the same as contracts signed by professional athletes—they agree to play for a team for a certain amount of time. After that time, the contract lapses and the parties can go their own way or negotiate a new contract. The same holds true for leases.

When a lease ends, the tenant and landlord must negotiate a new lease. Both parties have the freedom to accept or reject the terms and conditions offered by the other. Granted, the landlord is usually the one proposing new terms and conditions, but renters can make counter offers. If the tenant rejects the terms offered by the property owner, the tenant has made a choice. When a tenant is free to choose, we cannot call the result an act of force. Force negates choice.

It is true that sometimes none of the alternatives are desirable. For example, if the landlord proposes increasing the rent more than the tenant is comfortable paying, the tenant has alternatives, including reducing other expenses, getting a part-time job to increase his income, or moving. He may not like any of these options, but the fact is, he has options. And he is free to choose the option that is best for him.

The same is true of indirect displacement. If a low-income household vacates a home and the landlord increases rent beyond what other low-income households can afford, no force has been used and no displacement

has actually occurred. If the Smiths move out of a home and the Joneses can't afford the rent, the Joneses have not been displaced. They never occupied the housing unit.

This is not to say that displacement isn't real. It is real, but in regard to renters, it is not an issue of force. To equate voluntary choices and acts of force is to eliminate the difference between freedom and coercion, between being free to act on one's judgment and being forced to act contrary to one's judgment. However, in regard to homeowners, the story is different. The threat of force is often a cause of displacement for home owners. In this case, the "choice" offered to homeowners is: Your money or your house.

As a neighborhood gentrifies, property values generally rise, and sometimes dramatically. This causes property taxes to also rise. Low-income homeowners, as well as those on a fixed income, may struggle to pay the higher taxes. Faced with the "choice" of selling or having their property seized by taxing authorities for unpaid taxes, many "choose" to sell their home. However, the alternatives offered are the same as those offered by the armed robber who demands, "Your wallet or your life." Such demands arbitrarily eliminate one alternative. The victim of the robber wants a third alternative—his money and his life.

Similarly, the property owner wants another alternative—his money and his home.

The challenge is to find non-coercive ways to help these households. Two notable examples are volunteer organizations and non-profits.

Reducing Homeowner Displacement

Government demands payment of property taxes, regardless of an individual's desires or values. The property owner has no choice in the matter. Those who do not or cannot pay their taxes face the threat of foreclosure. The homeowner is forced to cede his property, whether it is money or his home. This is an injustice whether gentrification is occurring or not.

Reducing the displacement of homeowners can occur without coercive measures. One example from Portland, Oregon, is an organization called Taking Ownership PDX. Bringing together numerous contractors, realtors, neighbors, and businesses, the group focuses on repairs and maintenance of homes owned by low-income households in gentrifying neighborhoods. Its website states, "Together we renovate and revive Black-owned homes that have requested our help, with an emphasis on enabling Black homeowners to age in place...."[142]

Since its founding in July 2020, Taking Ownership has helped over fifty homeowners across the city. The organization has raised over half a million dollars and has 250 volunteers. This is an admittedly small effort, and it is limited to one city, but the same concept can be applied to anywhere. Those who are truly concerned about displacement can create their own organization to raise money and coordinate revitalization efforts. But the primary threat to homeowners is property taxes, and non-profits and volunteers can also help address that threat.

In Atlanta, a non-profit called Westside Future Fund assembled a coalition of businesses and philanthropists to create an "anti-displacement tax fund. (ADTF)." The organization's website says, "Once enrolled, the homeowner will have any increases in their existing property taxes paid by the ADTF program for up to 20 years."[143] Homeowners are not required to repay any taxes paid on their behalf. In the first year, the ADTF enrolled seventy homeowners from the neighborhoods it serves.

These volunteer efforts are laudable and will eventually save hundreds, if not thousands, of homeowners from displacement. But the broadest and most effective solution must come from government.

Legislators can and should address the issue of rising property taxes in gentrifying neighborhoods. They have the ability to reduce or limit the burden on homeowners in such neighborhoods. Doing so would allow property owners to retain their home while benefiting from the improvements brought by gentrification.

As one example of what legislators can do, many states offer a homestead exemption for homes that are occupied by the owner. While the details vary, they generally reduce the taxed value of a property. As one example, Texas offers a $25,000 exemption for school taxes. The state also limits increases in assessments on homesteads to 10 percent per year.

The same type of exemption could be applied to homeowners in gentrifying areas—a gentrification exemption. The exemption could be a fixed dollar amount, a limitation on increases in the assessed value of a property, or both. While a gentrification exemption would provide some relief from soaring property taxes, it would not prevent all displacement because of higher taxes. For example, if the assessed value could only increase 10 percent per year, such an increase would result in the assessed value rising nearly 80 percent in just five years.

A better solution is for legislators to freeze assessed values. As an example, Philadelphia offers homeowners 65 and older a program to freeze their property taxes if certain income requirements are met. A single person cannot make more than $27,500 a year to qualify, while a married couple can earn up to $35,500. Texas freezes school taxes for property owners over 65 (there are no income restrictions), and there is no reason that similar freezes can't be used more broadly. These two examples illustrate what government can and should do to reduce the displacement of homeowners in gentrifying neighborhoods.

Freezing property taxes is a much more effective remedy than tax exemptions. A tax freeze provides complete protection against tax increases and would make it much more likely that homeowners could stay in their home while the neighborhood around them improves. This could be done simply by removing the threat of coercion that taxation represents.

The real culprits in the displacement of homeowners are legislators. Rather than turning to coercive policies like inclusionary zoning, they should remove the primary source of homeowner displacement—soaring property taxes. And the same approach can be used to reduce the displacement of renters.

Reducing The Displacement Of Renters

When gentrification begins to occur in a neighborhood, the laws of supply and demand can result in increases in rents. As the neighborhood is revitalized, demand for housing increases. Even if new housing is built, the demand often exceeds the supply. When this occurs, rents for the existing housing increase. Low-income households cannot afford the increased rents and are displaced.

We have already seen how tax credits are used to incentivize developers to build low-income housing. Tax credits, tax exemptions, and tax freezes could be used to encourage property owners to keep their rents affordable for low-income families. The reduced property taxes would make up for the lower rents received. Tax credits could be made available to every rental property owner. The current policy limits tax credits to a small number of recipients and necessarily limits the number of units that can be built. Making tax credits available to all rental owners creates a much bigger pool for producing affordable housing. Such a program would properly allow a property owner to choose for himself whether to keep rents low or not.

Using tax reductions to encourage the provision of low-income housing is morally superior to inclusionary zoning. Using tax reductions is voluntary. Using inclusionary zoning is coercive.

Some argue that tax credits are a form of subsidy. However, there is a crucial distinction tax credits and subsidies. Tax credits allow individuals, businesses, and non-profits to keep more of their money, and that is a good thing. Subsidies take money from Peter to pay Paul, and that is just legalized robbery.

We will never eliminate all displacement. Individual housing needs and preferences change. Financial conditions change for better or worse. Sometimes, individuals simply want to live in a new environment. Whatever the reason, households move. This is neither good nor bad, but simply a fact that we must recognize and accept. But we can use non-coercive measures to reduce unwanted displacement.

The New Framework

We can take non-coercive steps to reduce displacement, particularly when it is not desired. We can implement tax freezes and other relief for property owners. We can expand tax credits for producing affordable housing to all property owners. Both of these require action on the part of government to reduce the burden on property owners.

To date, virtually all efforts to reduce displacement are founded on coercion. Whether it is using inclusionary zoning to compel developers to include low-income housing in their projects, using exclusionary zoning to prohibit redevelopment, or any variation, coercion is involved. Individuals, businesses, and developers are prohibited from using their property as they desire.

Sadly, while government officials across the country decry displacement, few propose non-coercive measures to reduce it. Instead, they follow the failed Progressive framework of forcing individuals to act in a prescribed manner, rather than protecting the freedom of individuals to choose the alternatives that best suit their needs and desires. If we truly want to reduce displacement, the place to start is by rejecting coercive measures. If we want to enable long-term residents to enjoy the benefits of gentrification, then we must reject any policy that disables others.

RESTORING ECONOMIC FREEDOM

Each year, governments at every level spend hundreds of billions of dollars on a variety of housing subsidy schemes for both renters and homebuyers. At the same time, governments have been imposing increasing regulations and controls on housing producers. These enormous expenditures and these rights-violating laws have not solved the housing crisis. They have made the situation worse.

We have seen how government policies artificially inflate the price of housing. Exclusionary zoning prohibits less expensive housing alternatives, such as duplexes and manufactured housing. We have also seen how government policies make it more difficult to earn a living and improve one's financial position. Because the affordability of housing involves more than just the price for a house or apartment, we must free both housing producers and housing consumers. We must take an integrated approach to housing and related policies if we want to achieve true justice. We must reject the Progressive framework that looks at issues in isolation, that fails to consider the long-term consequences of a policy. In its place, we must embrace the individualistic framework of the future.

Restoring Freedom Of Choice

If we want individuals to flourish, then they must be free to choose the values that will sustain and enrich their lives, as well as the means by which they will attain those values. They must be free to choose, and they must be free to act on their choices.

Freedom of choice means that we have alternatives, and we are not coerced to select one or another. Freedom of choice means that we can choose the alternative that we think will be in our best interest.

Freedom means an absence of coercion. An armed robber does not give us a choice when he declares, "Your wallet or your life." By waving a gun in your face, the robber eliminates one alternative: to retain both your wallet and your life. Freedom does not exist when alternatives are eliminated by coercive means. When coercion is used, we aren't free to choose. When coercion is used, we aren't free to act on our own judgment. Indeed, the purpose of coercion is to incentivize us to act contrary to our judgment. This is true no matter the number or variety of options the wielder of force offers. If we want to restore freedom of choice for both housing producers and housing consumers, then we must eliminate policies that coerce individuals to act contrary to their judgment.

Liberating individuals—all individuals—from the constraints of coercion enables each individual to live the life he chooses. Individuals will be free to produce, trade, and use material values as they deem best. When individuals are free to choose, they do not need permission from others. They are not threatened with harm if they do not act as others believe proper.

Government's proper purpose is not the provision of the values life requires. Government's proper purpose is the protection of our freedom to produce and earn the values that life requires. A proper government does not provide benefits to some at the expense of others. A proper government does not dictate what values can be produced, traded, or used. A proper government protects the freedom of individuals—all individuals—to produce, trade, and use material values as each judges best for his life. A proper government enables all while disabling nobody.

Production Has Primacy

Before any value can be consumed, it must first be produced. This is true of every value, from automobiles to televisions, from computers to housing. It is also true that, morally, each individual must produce before he can consume.

Alone on an island, it would be clear that your survival requires you to produce the values that will sustain your life. You would need to catch fish and game, pick berries and fruits, and build a shelter. You might need clothing and a hat to protect you from the sun. Until you act, the raw materials on the island will do nothing to sustain your life. Your ability to produce values will determine your ability to survive and thrive.

The same is true even when we live among others. In a moral society, our sustenance is not guaranteed. If we want to sustain and enhance our life, then we must produce or earn the values we need and desire. Obviously, we cannot produce every value that our life requires. We can, however, trade the values that we produce for the values that others produce. Those who produce have earned the values required to voluntarily trade with others to the benefit of everyone involved.

There are those who cannot or will not produce the values life requires. They depend on others, either through charity, welfare schemes, or criminal activities to provide the values that will sustain their lives. Charity is voluntary. Welfare and crime is coercive. Charity allows individuals to support the causes that are important to them. Welfare forces individuals to support causes that they may or may not support. Crime forces individuals to involuntarily cede property. Private charity allows individuals to share their production with those they deem worth. Welfare schemes and crime force individuals to share their production, regardless of their own desires and needs.

Justice demands that we grant to others that which they deserve, that which they have earned. One earns values by producing values. Those who do not produce values have not earned values. Private charity allows us to grant to others the values which we think they deserve. Welfare forces us to provide values to others regardless of our judgment.

Many of the policies that we have examined have been founded the premise that values do not have to be produced or earned. Those policies are founded on the premise that values can and should be attained by hook or by crook—by any means necessary. And so, government uses subsidies to incentivize the production of values that it favors, such as single-family homes, solar panels, electric cars, roads, and affordable housing. When subsidies aren't effective, government resorts to coercive measures, such as zoning, minimum wage, occupational licensing

Fundamentally, the housing shortage is a supply shortage. America needs more housing, and that requires more production. If we want to enable each individual to obtain safe, decent, and affordable housing, then we must recognize the primacy of production. We must unshackle housing producers and remove the arbitrary restrictions and regulations that prevent them from producing the housing our nation desperately needs.

Freeing Housing Producers

As we have seen, housing producers are shackled with a plethora of regulations, controls, dictates, and prohibitions. Virtually every aspect of housing production is subject to some form of regulation. Construction cannot begin until permission is obtained from government officials. Once construction begins, a project is subject to regular inspections by government officials who can shut down a project until their demands are met. A final inspection is often required before occupancy will be permitted. All of this adds to the time and cost of building new housing.

We have already examined the benefits of eliminating exclusionary zoning. While this would be a major step towards freeing housing producers, other restrictions must also be eliminated. The most notable are environmental regulations and building codes. As with zoning, there are non-coercive means to prevent pollution and ensure that buildings are safely constructed.

No rational person wants polluted air and water. Neither is conducive to human well-being. However, the defenders of environmental controls and regulations on individuals, businesses, and industry present us with a false alternative. If we accept the controls and regulations, we will have clean air and water. If we reject the controls and regulations, we will have polluted air and water. But there is an alternative—the recognition and protection of property rights.

If an individual or business damages the property of others, the guilty party is financially and morally liable for damages. If you cause an automobile accident, you are responsible for repairing the other vehicle. If you dump toxic chemicals on a neighbor's land, you are responsible for remediating the damage. Because they move, air and water present certain challenges in the application of this principle. But those challenges can be overcome.

We have seen how one application of property rights —nuisance laws—protects individuals from activities that interfere with the peaceful use of their property. We saw how that principle applied to smoke. An individual can generate smoke so long as he does not interfere with others' using their property. The same principle applies to any air or water borne pollutant. If an individual or business can generate and dispose of pollutants without damaging the property of others or interfering with their use of that property, no damage has been done.

It may be the case that the emissions of one factory do not cause damage to other's property, but the cumulative effect of many factories is damaging. If this could be objectively proven, then it would be appropriate for government to intervene. However, the justification is not the protection of the environment, but rather, the protection of property rights.

The advocates of environmental regulations are not attempting to protect property rights. Their goal is to leave nature unsullied by human activity. And to achieve that, then want to restrict, control, and often prohibit, activities that produce values. The frantic calls to eliminate the use of fossil fuels are one example.

Fossil fuels are the lifeblood of a modern society. Oil, gas, and coal provide the abundant, affordable, and reliable energy that we need to live and produce. Yet, government continually restricts and prohibits the production of fossil fuels, such as banning drilling offshore or denying permits to build a pipeline.

Protecting the environment from productive human activities dramatically restricts the freedom of builders and developers to produce more housing. Large areas throughout the country are off-limits for development, even when demand for housing is rising in those areas. Regulations to protect "wetlands" and "environmentally sensitive" areas similarly remove a significant portion of land from development.

We can have an abundance of affordable housing, but we must remove the restrictions—all of the restrictions—that prevent housing producers from building the housing that America wants and needs. And that includes environmental regulations that prohibit development.

Just as many believe that environmental regulations are necessary to keep air and water clean, many believe that government enforced building codes are necessary to ensure that housing is properly built. But as with pollution, there are non-coercive means to achieve desirable ends.

Rational individuals and businesses do not want to damage others' property, whether through pollution or any other means. Nor do rational individuals and businesses want to construct buildings that are unsafe. Many builders and contractors already build housing that goes beyond the requirements of their local building codes.

In the absence of government building codes, there are numerous ways that homebuyers can ensure that they are buying a house that is safe and properly constructed. One obvious way is the builder's reputation. With the Internet, it's never been easier to read reviews and communicate with those who have used a product or service provider.

Insurance companies have a vested interest in ensuring that buildings are safe and properly built. If damage occurs, the insurance company is financially liable for repairs. They will establish criteria that builders and developers must meet to remain insured. Indeed, my insurance company regularly inspects my rental properties to ensure that the homes are being maintained. Insurance companies might require periodic inspections during construction, some form of voluntary certification, or other measures to minimize their exposure to claims.

Many industries and manufacturers use voluntary certifications. For example, Underwriters Laboratories (UL) tests and certifies electrical products. Because of UL's rigorous standards and stellar reputation, some products are very difficult to sell without the organization's certification. Another example is *Good Housekeeping*. Since 1909, the magazine has been testing and approving a variety of household products. As with the UL mark, the *Good Housekeeping* Seal of Approval is often considered necessary for a product's success. There is no reason to believe that similar types of certifications won't develop in the absence of government building codes. Indeed, the manufacturers of many building materials, such as siding and roofing, offer training and certification for installers.

Such certifications would give both producers and consumers more choices and options. For example, a builder could choose which agency to certify his homes, or he could choose to forgo certification entirely. So long as he does not claim a certification that he does not possess, he has violated nobody's rights. And by refraining from certification, he will likely reduce his costs and better enable his business to build housing that is affordable to low- and moderate income households.

Most builders offer upgrades to homebuyers. The builder offers a standard home and then allows the buyer to upgrade or add various features. This allows the buyer to get what he wants and can afford. If the basic "economy" home best suits his needs, he is able to select it, rather than be required to buy a home with features he doesn't want or need. Building codes often add significant costs to new construction by mandating energy efficient appliances and windows, hard-wired smoke alarms, and similar features that homeowners may or may not want or be able to afford. If the buyer has options, he can select those options that best suit his needs and desires. He will more easily find housing that is affordable.

Some homebuyers will choose to buy a certified home. Some will opt for an uncertified home because of the lower cost. Again, consumers will have the option of choosing which certification standards best meet their needs and budget. When both producers and consumers are free to choose, both will benefit.

Government building codes remove many choices from both housing producers and housing consumers. Such codes prohibit builders and developers from offering housing that has lesser quality features, and therefore, a lower selling price. This doesn't mean that they will build unsafe housing. It does mean that they can choose to offer a range of products to home buyers, just as the manufacturers of automobiles, computers, televisions, and virtually every consumer product do.

Freeing housing producers will enable them to find innovative ways to produce more affordable housing. And freeing housing consumers will enable them to more easily afford the housing that they want and desire.

Freeing Housing Consumers

Freeing housing producers will increase the supply of housing and will help reduce prices. However, if we do not simultaneously free housing consumers, safe and decent housing will remain unaffordable for many Americans. Unless housing consumers are free to produce as they think best, their ability to trade for the housing they desire will be restricted. Their ability to consume will remain limited.

Consumption can only occur after a value has been produced. As producers, we create the values that others want and need. As consumers, we trade for the values that others have produced to satisfy our desires and needs. Our ability to trade for those values is determined by our production. The more that we produce, the more that we can trade. And the more that we can trade, the more that we can consume.

Just as government policies place shackles on housing producers, other policies place shackles on those who want to gain job skills, start a business, or obtain certain jobs. Those shackles prevent individuals from gaining experience, developing new skills, and increasing their earning potential. Those shackles prevent individuals from improving their productive capacity. It is not enough to enable housing producers to produce more housing. We must also enable everyone to produce more. Only by producing more can individuals consume more of anything, including housing. Sadly, a variety of policies make it more difficult for individuals to produce more.

Consider a high school student who wants to get a job. He has no job skills or work experience. He has little to offer an employer other than a willingness to work. But employers often can't afford to pay an inexperienced, unskilled worker the minimum dictated by the government. The student is unable to find a job and gain valuable experience. Instead, he enters adulthood with no marketable skills.

However, absent minimum wage laws, the student might decide that it would be in his best interest to work for a low wage, such as $5 per hour. He still lives at home and doesn't need much money. Indeed, he needs experience more than money, and he is willing to work for less in order to obtain that experience. Nobody is harmed if he works for $5 an hour. Both he and his employer benefit. The employee earns a small amount of money, but he gains invaluable job experience. The employer gets a worker that he previously couldn't afford.

When we prohibit individuals from working for a wage less than that permitted by law, we deny them opportunities. We deny them the freedom to choose what employment terms are acceptable to them. If an individual believes that working for $5 an hour is better than not working, there is no moral reason to prohibit him from doing so. When that opportunity is denied today, he cannot obtain the experience and skills that will enable him to earn a higher wage tomorrow. Minimum wage laws are not the only impediments to improving one's financial situation.

Consider a young immigrant who learned the art of African hair braiding from her grandmother. Possessing few other skills, she decides to open a business offering hair braiding services. She has the requisite skills and has practiced the art on countless relatives, friends, and neighbors in her native country. However, in many states, she must obtain a cosmetology license before she could legally offer such services.

The cost of attending a cosmetology school is beyond her ability to pay. Besides, few schools offer any classes in hair braiding. Even if she could afford it, attending cosmetology school would simply be a waste of her time. Jestina Clayton, whose story we very briefly examined in Chapter 8, is an example.

A native of Sierra Leone, she had learned hair braiding as a child. After moving to the United States at the age of 18, she went to college, got married, and had several children. After graduating college, she discovered that the entry level jobs that she was offered would barely cover the cost of child-care. She decided to start a hair braiding business in her home. She marketed the new business on a local website. And then one day she received an email from a stranger that declared, "It is illegal in the state of Utah to do any form of extensions without a valid cosmetology license. Please delete your ad, or you will be reported."[144] Unable to afford the two years and $16,000 it would require to obtain a license, she closed her business.

Clayton subsequently sued the State of Utah, and in 2012 a federal court ruled in her favor, stating,

> The State does not know which schools, if any, teach African hair braiding; how many hours, if any, of African hair braiding instruction are available at those unknown schools; or whether the unknown number of hours of instruction at those unknown schools are mandatory or elective. ...

> Utah's cosmetology/barbering licensing scheme is so disconnected from the practice of African hairbraiding, much less from whatever minimal threats to public health and safety are connected to braiding, that to premise Jestina's right to earn a living by braiding hair on that scheme is wholly irrational and a violation of her constitutionally protected rights.[145]

While Clayton was able to resume her business, her story illustrates the destructive character of occupational licensing. Many do not have the time or desire to fight licensing laws, and they simply give up their dream of starting a business and improving their life.

Enterprising individuals like Clayton often possess skills that others are willing to pay for. However, in many professions occupational licensing prevents them from offering their services without first obtaining the government's permission to earn a living. Such prohibitions are particularly debilitating to the ambitious poor—individuals who lack the money and cannot afford to spend years in school. These individuals are unable to start a business or enter the profession of their choosing with the goal of improving their financial position.

Eliminating occupational licensing does not mean that consumers will be left to the mercy of charlatans and the incompetent. As with builders, private certification could assure consumers that the professionals they hire are well-trained and reputable. Many industries, include automotive services and computer repair facilities, offer such certifications, either through a trade organization or a product manufacturer.

With voluntary certification, service providers could choose which certifications to obtain, or none at all. And consumers would be free to hire either certified or non-certified providers. Each provider could choose what to offer, and each consumer could choose what to purchase based on his own preferences and budget.

Similarly, pro-union laws compel employers to negotiate with labor unions and essentially force workers to join unions if they seek certain jobs. Such laws restrict the freedom of businesses to hire and pay as they deem best and restrict the freedom of workers to negotiate terms and conditions more to their liking. For example, a young, single adult may choose to forgo health insurance or accept a lower wage in order to secure a job. An employer might offer different benefit packages and base a worker's pay on the package selected.

Absent pro-union laws, both employers and employees would have the freedom to choose the terms and conditions of employment that are mutually beneficial. If we want to make housing more affordable, we must eliminate the barriers that make it more difficult to earn a living.

The New Framework

If we want to enable individuals to afford better housing, then we must restore economic freedom to both producers and consumers. We must remove the barriers that prevent producers from offering housing alternatives. We must remove the barriers that prevent individuals from improving their financial position.

Removing barriers enables individuals—each individual —to choose the course of his own life. That is the moral way to address the housing crisis. That is the moral way to achieve housing justice.

THE FRAMEWORK OF THE FUTURE

If we truly wish to solve the affordable housing problem, then we cannot cling to the collectivist framework that created and then exacerbated the problem. We need to think about housing, and all related issues, in a fresh way. We need to embrace a new framework.

It is impossible to predict the innovative solutions to the housing crisis that individuals will discover. When individuals are free to think "out of the box" and then act on their ideas, mankind moves forward. Innovators throughout history have been scorned and ridiculed for ideas that others thought crazy.

As an example, Thomas Edison was derided as a fool who knew nothing about electricity when he proposed inventing an electric light bulb. Because he was free to act on his idea, even when the "experts" thought him delusional, he succeeded and everyone benefitted, including his detractors. Patillo Higgins was ridiculed for proclaiming that oil existed in a salt dome in Beaumont, Texas. Again, the "experts" denounced his idea. Like Edison, Higgins was free to act on his idea. When he succeeded and oil gushed from Spindletop, the Texas oil industry was born.

But what would have happened if Edison, Higgins, and all of history's innovators were not free to act on their ideas? What if they first had to secure the permission of government officials? What if they could not act on their own judgment, but could only act as a democratic majority deemed appropriate? It is unlikely that we would have the electric light bulb, a vibrant energy economy in Texas, or any of the countless values that make our lives better.

The framework of the future is about freedom. It is about restoring freedom to housing producers and housing consumers—to everyone. The framework of the future is about enabling individuals—every individual—to pursue his vision of happiness. It is about enabling individuals to earn the housing that they desire.

We have a choice. We can cling to the failed framework of the past and present. If we do so, we cannot rationally expect different results. Or, we can embrace a new framework, a framework that looks at the big picture and empowers individuals to live flourishing lives. Which do you choose?

INDEX

---

[1]. James Edwin Creighton, *Studies in Speculative Philosophy* (New York, Macmillan, 1925), pp49-50.

[2]. Arthur A. Ekrich, Jr., *Progressivism in America*, (New York, Franklin Watts, 1974), p151.

[3]. Quoted in Elizabeth Schleber Lowry, The Seybert Report: Rhetoric, Rationale, and the Problem of Psi Research, (Palgrave Macmillan, 2017), p13.

[4]. Quoted in Leonard Peikoff, *Ominous Parallels*, (Stein and Day, New York, 1982) p127.

[5]. John W. Burgess, *The Foundations of Political Science*, (Columbia University Press, New York, 1933), p101.

[6]. Ekrich, op. cit., p26.

[7]. Josiah Royce, *The World and the Individual*, (New York, The MacMillan Company, 1923) p249.

[8]. Ekrich, op. cit., p158.

[9]. Leonard Peikoff, *Objectivism: The Philosophy of Ayn Rand*, (Penguin Books, New York, 1991), p123.

[10]. Peikoff, op. cit., *Ominous Parallels*, p129.

[11]. Patrick Range McDonald, "Californians Can't Afford Rent - It's Still Too Damn High!," City Watch, May 6, 2021, https://www.citywatchla.com/index.php/cw/los-angeles/21691-californians-can-t-afford-rent-it-s-still-too-damn-high, accessed September 20, 2022.

[12]. "Los Angeles California Residential Rent and Rental Statistics, Department of Numbers, https://www.deptofnumbers.com/rent/california/los-angeles-county/, accessed January 15, 2022.

[13]. "Los Angeles, CA," Data USA, https://datausa.io/profile/geo/los-angeles-ca, accessed January 15, 2022.

[14]. "San Francisco, CA," Data USA, https://www.deptofnumbers.com/rent/california/san-francisco/, accessed January 15, 2022.

[15]. "San Francisco, CA," Data USA, https://datausa.io/profile/geo/san-francisco-ca, accessed January 15, 2022.

[16]. Don Watkins and Yaron Brook, *Equal is Unfair*, (St. Martin's Press, New York, 2017), p42.

[17]. Betsy McCaughey, "Biden's 'infrastructure' plan wages war on the suburban dream," *New York Post*, May 17, 2021, https://nypost.com/2021/05/17/bidens-infrastructure-plan-wages-war-on-the-suburban-dream/, accessed September 20, 2022.

[18]. "Buchanan v. Warley," United States Supreme Court, 245 U.S. 60 (1917).

[19]. Jay Caspian Kang, "Want to Solve the Housing Crisis? Take Over Hotels," *The New York Times*, August 19, 2021, https://www.nytimes.com/2021/08/19/opinion/housing-crisis-hotels.html, accessed September 20, 2022.

[20]. Emily Badger and Bui Quoctrung, "Cities Start to Question an American Ideal: A House With a Yard on Every Lot," *The New York Times*, June 18, 2019, https://www.nytimes.com/interactive/2019/06/18/upshot/cities-across-america-question-single-family-zoning.html, accessed September 20, 2022.

[21]. Quoted in Richard Rothstein, *The Color of Law*, (Liveright Publishing, New York, 2017), p52.

[22]. "What is the Purpose of Zoning?" Millman National Land Services, https://prs3.com/3-reasons-zoning-laws-are-needed/, accessed September 21, 2022.

[23]. "Purposes of Zoning," Tyler Topics, http://tylertopics.com/cityhallcommons/topiclist/c130.zoning.html, accessed September 21, 2022.

[24]. Sarah Crump, "Fixing Greater Boston's housing crisis starts with legalizing apartments near transit," Brookings Institution, October 14, 2020, https://www.brookings.edu/research/fixing-greater-bostons-housing-crisis-starts-with-legalizing-apartments-near-transit/, accessed September 21, 2022.

[25]. Richard N. Maier, "The Cost of Regulation; The Effect of Municipal Land Use Regulations on Housing Affordability," http://austintexas.gov/sites/default/files/files/Planning/CodeNEXT/Effects_of_Regulation_on_Housing_Affordability-RMaier.pdf, accessed September 10, 2022.

[26]. "Austin Home Prices and Values," Zillow.com, https://

www.zillow.com/austin-tx/home-values/, accessed November 19, 2017.

[27]. Russell Hokanson, Reagan Dunn and Samuel L. Anderson, "Misguided Land-use Regulations Push Middle Class out of King County," *The Seattle Times*, April 9, 2008, https://www.seattletimes.com/opinion/misguided-land-use-regulations-push-middle-class-out-of-king-county/, accessed September 10, 2022.

[28]. Rothstein, op. cit., p94.

[29]. William Cresap, "The Real Estate and Stock Market During the Great Depression: Construction Permit Growth as a Leading Economic Indicator for Stock Returns" (2017). *CMC Senior Theses*. 1604, http://scholarship.claremont.edu/cmc_theses/1604, accessed September 21, 2022.

[30]. "Community Reinvestment Act," https://www.federalreserve.gov/consumerscommunities/cra_about.htm, accessed September 21, 2022.

[31]. Alicia H. Munnell, Lynn Elaine Browne, James McEneaney, and Geoffrey M.B. Tootell, "Mortgage Lending in Boston: Interpreting HMDA Data," Federal Reserve Bank of Boston, https://www.bostonfed.org/publications/research-department-working-paper/1992/mortgage-lending-in-boston-interpreting-hmda-data.aspx, accessed September 21, 2022.

[32]. Ibid.

[33]. "Assessing the Public Costs and Benefits of Fannie Mae and Freddie Mac," Congressional Budget Office, May 1996, https://www.cbo.gov/publication/10339, accessed September 21, 2022.

[34]. John Allison, *The Financial Crisis and the Free Market Cure*, (McGraw-Hill, New York, 2013), p57.

[35]. Timothy Howard, *The Mortgage Wars*, (McGraw-Hill, New York, 2014), p257.

[36]. Ibid.

[37]. Allison, op. cit., p14.

[38]. Allison, op. cit., p51.

[39]. Howard, op. cit., p257.

[40]. "Monetary Policy," Investopedia, https://www.investopedia.com/terms/m/monetarypolicy.asp, accessed September 21, 2022.

[41]. Howard, op. cit., p169.

[42]. "NAR defends mortgage interest

deduction," Inman, https://www.inman.com/2010/12/01/nar-defends-mortgage-interest-deduction/, accessed September 21, 2022.

[43]. "NAHB Urges Congress to Enact Policies to Help Builders Boost Housing Production," National Association of Home Builders, July 14, 2021, https://www.nahb.org/blog/2021/07/nahb-urges-congress-to-enact-policies-to-help-builders-boost-housing-production/, accessed September 21, 2022.

[44]. Allison, op. cit., p20.

[45]. Allison, op. cit., p56.

[46]. Ibid.

[47]. "What We Do," Securities Exchange Commission, https://www.sec.gov/about/what-we-do

[48]. Allison, op. cit., p152.

[49]. Owen D. Gutfreund, *Twentieth-Century Sprawl: Highways and the Reshaping of the American Landscape*, (Oxford University Press, New York, 2004), p14.

[50]. Gutfreund, op. cit., p26.

[51]. Gutfreund, op. cit., p34.

[52]. Gutfreund, op. cit., p41.

[53]. Jean Edward Smith, *(2012). Eisenhower in War and Peace*, (Random House, New York, 2012), p. 652-653.

[54]. Rothstein, op. cit., p131.

[55]. Quoted in Joseph Stromberg, "Highways gutted American cities. So why did they build them?, Vox, May 11, 2016, https://www.vox.com/2015/5/14/8605917/highways-interstate-cities-history, accessed September 22, 2022.

[56]. Ibid.

[57]. Gutfreund, op. cit., pp228-29.

[58]. Matthew Desmond, *Evicted: Poverty and Profit in the American City*,(Broadway Books, New York, 2016), p78.

[59]. Desmond, op. cit., p127.

[60]. Sterling Johnson and Jennifer Bennetech, "Biden's plan could be disastrous for low-income homeowners in Philly," The Philadeplphia Enquirer, April 13, 2021, https://www.inquirer.com/opinion/commentary/low-income-housing-philadelphia-biden-american-jobs-plan-20210413.html, accessed September 22, 2022.

[61]. "Blooming Nonsense: IJ Files Suit to Uproot Florist Licensing Law," Institute for Justice, April 6, 2010, https://ij.org/ll/blooming-nonsense-ij-files-suit-to-uproot-

florist-licensing-law/, accessed September 22, 2022.

[62]. Rothstein, op. cit., p158

[63]. David Deerson, "California's new laws are tackling the housing shortage," Pacific Legal Foundation, September 8, 2021, https://pacificlegal.org/californias-new-laws-tackling-housing-shortage/, accessed September 22, 2022.

[64]. "Governor Newsom Signs Historic Legislation to Boost California's Housing Supply and Fight the Housing Crisis," Office of Governor Gavin Newsome, September 16, 2021 https://www.gov.ca.gov/2021/09/16/governor-newsom-signs-historic-legislation-to-boost-californias-housing-supply-and-fight-the-housing-crisis/, accessed September 22, 2022.

[65]. "Supervisors Trample Public Interest in Approving Trabuco Tract Development," SaddlebackCanyonConservancy.com, http://www.saddlebackcanyons.org/editorial.html, accessed March 26, 2013.

[66]. Erin B. Logan, "Biden targets housing rules that hurt low-income earners. Will the suburbs buy in?" Los Angeles Times, May 19, 2021, https://www.latimes.com/politics/story/2021-05-19/bidens-infrastructure-plan-targets-exclusionary-zoning, accessed September 22, 2022.

[67]. Betsy McCaughey, "Joe Biden's disastrous plans for America's suburbs," New York Post, July 21, 2020, https://nypost.com/2020/07/21/joe-bidens-disastrous-plans-for-americas-suburbs/, accessed September 22, 2022.

[68]. David Imbroscio, "Say It Ain't So, Joe: Biden's Ill-Advised Plan to Eliminate Exclusionary Zoning," Shelter Force, January 28, 2021 https://shelterforce.org/2021/01/28/say-it-aint-so-joe-bidens-ill-advised-plan-to-eliminate-exclusionary-zoning/, accessed September 23, 2022.

[69]. Dejan Eskic, "The Impact of High-Density Apartments on Surrounding Single-Family Home Values in Suburban Salt Lake County," Kem C. Gardner Institute, February 2021, https://gardner.utah.edu/wp-content/uploads/HighDensity-Feb2021.pdf?x71849, accessed September 23, 2022.

[70]. "Measuring the Early Impact of Eliminating Single-Family Zoning on Minneapolis Property Values," American Planning Association, https://www.planning.org/blog/9219556/measuring-the-early-impact-of-eliminating-single-family-zoning-on-minneapolis-property-values/, accessed September 23, 2022.

[71]. While there is no such thing as "tenants' rights," the term is widely used in discussions of housing policies. I will use the more accurate term "tenant protections."

[72]. Jen Deerinwater, "What Does Housing Justice Really Mean?" Rewire News Group, July 31, 2020, https://rewirenewsgroup.com/article/2020/07/31/what-does-housing-justice-really-mean/, accessed September 23, 2022.

[73]. "To solve homelessness, California should declare a right to housing," Los Angeles Times, June 6, 2021, https://www.latimes.com/opinion/story/2021-06-06/homelessness-right-to-housing-human-right-reimagine-california, accessed September 23, 2022.

[74]. "Housing Justice National Platform for a Homes Guarantee," Housing Justice Platform, https://www.housingjusticeplatform.org/, accessed September 23, 2022.

[75]. "Ban the Box," Wikipedia, https://en.wikipedia.org/wiki/Ban_the_Box, accessed September 23, 2022.

[76]. Libby Solomon, "Montgomery County could "ban the box" for rental housing applications," Greater Greater Washington, December 16, 2020, https://ggwash.org/view/79893/montgomery-county-could-ban-the-box-for-rental-housing-applications, accessed September 23, 2022.

[77]. Sophie Nieto-Munoz, "Murphy signs historic law banning N.J. landlords from asking renters about criminal records," https://www.nj.com/politics/2021/06/murphy-signs-law-banning-housing-discrimination-against-renters-with-criminal-records.html, accessed September 23, 2022.

[78]. Coco Papy, "Savannahians with criminal histories deserve same opportunities afforded other citizens," *Savannah Morning News*, May 19, 2021, https://www.savannahnow.com/story/opinion/2021/05/19/discrimination-housing-and-employment-practices-punish-those-criminal-records/5125604001/, accessed September 23, 2022.

[79]. Annie Howard, "Fighting No-Fault Evictions with a Just Cause Ordinance," Shelter Force, December 11, 2020, https://shelterforce.org/2020/12/11/fighting-no-fault-evictions-with-a-just-cause-ordinance/, accessed September 23, 2022.

[80]. David Brand, "NYC Tenants Reignite Push for 'Good Cause' Eviction Protections, Despite Landlord Opposition," City Limits, October 20,2021, https://citylimits.org/2021/10/20/nyc-tenants-reignite-push-for-good-cause-eviction-protections-

despite-landlord-opposition/, accessed September 23, 2022.

[81]. "Letter to the Editor: Support Good Cause Eviction Legislation," The Ithaca Voice, November 8, 2021, https://ithacavoice.com/2021/11/letter-to-the-editor-support-good-cause-eviction-legislation/, accessed September 23, 2022.

[82]. "Renter's Choice puts cash back in the hands of renters," Renter Choice, https://www.renterchoice.org/, accessed September 23, 2022.

[83]. John Phelan, "81% of economists agree that rent controls are bad policy," American Experiment, December 14, 2018, https://www.americanexperiment.org/81-of-economists-agree-that-rent-controls-are-bad-policy/, accessed September 23, 2022.

[84]. "The High Cost of Rent Control," National Multifamily Housing Council, https.://www.nmhc.org/news/articles/the-high-cost-of-rent-control/, accessed September 23, 2022.

[85]. Ibid.

[86]. Ibid.

[87]. Rebecca Diamond, "What does economic evidence tell us about the effects of rent control?" Brookings Institution, October 18, 2018 https://www.brookings.edu/research/what-does-economic-evidence-tell-us-about-the-effects-of-rent-control accessed September 24, 2022.

[88]. Ibid.

[89]. Ibid.

[90]. Cea Weaver, "There's no Denying the Data: Rent Control Works," The Hill, September 24, 2021, https://thehill.com/opinion/finance/573841-theres-no-denying-the-data-rent-control-works, accessed September 24, 2022.

[91]. Jake Blumgart, "In Defense of Rent Control," Pacific Standard, June 14, 2017, https://psmag.com/economics/in-defense-of-rent-control, accessed September 24, 2022.

[92]. Henry Hazlett, Economics in One Lesson, (Arlington House, New York, 1979), p33.

[93]. (Hire Purchase Agreements: Definition, How They Work, Pros and Cons," Investopedia, February 22, 2022, https://www.investopedia.com/terms/s/subsidy.asp, accessed September 24, 2022.

[94]. Joseph Kast, "How One of the Most Renowned Architects in History (Accidentally) Exposed the Problems of Central Planning," Foundation for Economic Education, May 26, 2022, https://fee.org/articles/how-one-of-the-most-renowned-

architects-in-history-accidentally-exposed-the-problems-of-central-planning/, accessed September 24, 2022.

[95]. Bernie Sanders, "NEWS: Sanders and Ocasio-Cortez Rollout Green New Deal for Public Housing Act," United States Senate, April 19, 2021, https://www.sanders.senate.gov/press-releases/news-sanders-and-ocasio-cortez-rollout-green-new-deal-for-public-housing-act/, accessed September 24, 2022.

[96]. Ibid

[97]. Ibid

[98]. Hazlett, op. cit., p35.

[99]. Kristian Hernández, "Biden Wants to Offer More Housing Vouchers. Many Landlords Won't Accept Them." Pew, May 12, 2021, https://www.pewtrusts.org/en/research-and-analysis/blogs/stateline/2021/05/12/biden-wants-to-offer-more-housing-vouchers-many-landlords-wont-accept-them, accessed September 24, 2022.

[100]. Ibid.

[101]. Ibid.

[102]. Gianpaolo Baiocchi and H. Jacob Carlson, "Housing is a Social Good," Boston Review, June 2, 2021, https://bostonreview.net/class-inequality-law-justice/gianpaolo-baiocchi-h-jacob-carlson-housing-social-good, accessed September 24, 2022.

[103]. Ibid.

[104]. Ibid.

[105]. Ibid.

[106]. Zach Wichter, "Path to increasing minority homeownership goes through Fannie and Freddie," Bank Rate, September 8, 2021, https://www.bankrate.com/mortgages/fannie-and-freddie-goals-for-minority-mortgage-lending/, accessed September 24, 2022.

[107]. "Cuomo Announces Action to Provide $2.4 trillion in Mortgages for Affordable Housing for 28.1 Families," U.S. Department of Housing and Urban Development, July 29, 1999, https://archives.hud.gov/news/1999/pr99-131.html, accessed September 24, 2022.

[108]. "Neighborhood Homes Investment Act," Neighborhood Homes Coalition, https://neighborhoodhomesinvestmentact.org/s/NHIA-Summary-September-2021.docx, accessed September 24, 2022.

[109]. "Neighborhood Homes Investment Act 2022 FAQs," National Council of State Housing Agencies, March 12, 2022, https://www.ncsha.org/wp-content/uploads/Neighborhood-Homes-Investment-Act-FAQs-2022.pdf, accessed September 24, 2022.

[110]. "Secretary Carson Terminates 2015 AFFH Rule," U.S. Department of Housing and Urban Development, July 23, 2020, https://www.hud.gov/press/press_releases_media_advisories/hud_no_20_109, accessed September 24, 2022.

[111]. "In play for suburban votes, Trump rescinds Obama-era fair housing rule," Reuters, July 29, 2020, https://www.reuters.com/article/usa-trump-suburbs-idUKL2N2F02NC, accessed September 16, 2022.

[112]. "Downpayment Toward Equity Act of 2021," National Council of State Housing Agencies, July 16, 2021, https://www.ncsha.org/wp-content/uploads/Summary-of-DPA-Toward-Equity-Act-of-2021.pdf, accessed September 24, 2022.

[113]. Jacob Passy, "Is renting cheaper than owning a home? Here's the answer in America's 50 biggest cities," Market Watch, May 21, 2021, https://www.marketwatch.com/story/is-renting-cheaper-than-owning-a-home-heres-the-answer-in-americas-50-biggest-cities-11621440360, accessed September 24, 2022.

[114]. "Latest Build Back Better Package Retains Commitment to Unlocking Possibilities Program," Up for Growth, November 4, 2021, https://www.upforgrowth.org/news/latest-build-back-better-package-retains-commitment-unlocking-possibilities-program, accessed September 24, 2022.

[115]. "About Us," Up for Growth, https://www.upforgrowth.org/about-us, accessed September 24, 2022.

[116]. "Latest Build Back Better Package Retains Commitment to Unlocking Possibilities Program," https://www.upforgrowth.org/news/latest-build-back-better-package-retains-commitment-unlocking-possibilities-program, accessed September 24, 2022.

[117]. "Home Investment Partnerships Program," U.S. Department of Housing and Urban Development, September 13, 2022, https://www.hud.gov/program_offices/comm_planning/home, accessed September 24, 2022.

[118]. "Gentrification and Neighborhood Revitalization: What's the Difference?" National Low Income Housing Coalition, April 5, 2019, https://nlihc.org/

resource/gentrification-and-neighborhood-revitalization-whats-difference, accessed September 25, 2022.

[119]. "Understanding Gentrification and Displacement," University of Texas, https://sites.utexas.edu/gentrificationproject/understanding-gentrification-and-displacement/, accessed September 25, 2022.

[120]. "What Are Gentrification and Displacement," Urban Displacement Project, https://www.urbandisplacement.org/about/what-are-gentrification-and-displacement/ accessed September 25, 2022.

[121]. "Gentrification and Neighborhood Revitalization: What's the Difference?" op.cit.

[122]. Shane Phillips, Michael Manville, Michael Lens, "The Effect of Market-Rate Development on Neighborhood Rents," UCLA Lewis Center for Regional Studies, February 17, 2021, https://escholarship.org/uc/item/5d00z61m?, accessed September 25, 2022.

[123]. Steve Chiotakis, "Does new housing raise nearby rents? Researchers and community leaders have differing views," KCRW, May 18, 2021, https://www.kcrw.com/news/shows/greater-la/la-street-housing/gentrification-rent, accessed September 25, 2022.

[124]. Hannah Alani, "After Decades In Wicker Park, Senior Homeowners Forced Out By Skyrocketing Property Taxes: 'This Neighborhood Has Broken My Heart'," Block Club Chicago, March 23, 2021, https://blockclubchicago.org/2021/03/23/after-decades-in-wicker-park-senior-homeowners-forced-out-by-skyrocketing-property-taxes-this-neighborhood-has-broken-my-heart/, accessed September 25, 2022.

[125]. Ibid.

[126]. Irene Vazquez, "In Houston's Third Ward, Community Groups are fighting for Equitable Development," *Texas Observer*, https://www.texasobserver.org/in-houstons-third-ward-community-groups-are-fighting-for-equitable-development/, accessed September 25, 2022.

[127]. Jecorey Arthur, "Historically Black Neighborhoods, Jecorey Arthur, https://www.jecoreyarthur.com/hbn, accessed September 25, 2022.

[128]. "Market Failure: What it is in Economics, Common Types and Causes," Investopedia, December 6, 2021, https://www.investopedia.com/terms/m/marketfailure.asp,

accessed September 25, 2022.

[129]. Ian Stephens, "Free Market will not Solve Housing Crisis," The Daily Californian, September 22, 2020, https://www.dailycal.org/2020/09/22/free-market-will-not-solve-housing-crisis, accessed September 25, 2022.

[130]. Zelda Bronstein, "When Affordable Housing Meets Free-market Fantasy," Dissent, November 17, 2017, https://www.dissentmagazine.org/online_articles/hsieh-moretti-affordable-housing-free-market-fantasy, accessed September 25, 2022.

[131]. Patrick Range McDonald, "Trickle-Down Housing is a Failure—Here's What You Need to Know," City Watch, May 27, 2021, https://www.citywatchla.com/index.php/cw/los-angeles/21816-trickle-down-housing-is-a-failure-here-s-what-you-need-to-know, accessed September 25, 2022.

[132]. Evan Mast, "The Effect of New Market-Rate Housing Construction on the Low-Income Housing Market," W.E. Upjohn Institute for Employment Research, July 1, 2019, https://research.upjohn.org/up_workingpapers/307/, accessed September 25, 2022.

[133]. "Ranked Single Family Second Quarter 2022," National Association of Realtors, https://cdn.nar.realtor/sites/default/files/documents/metro-home-prices-q2-2022-ranked-median-single-family-2022-08-11.pdf, accessed September 25, 2022.

[134]. Nick Halter, "Minneapolis move to legalize triplexes shows little impact," https://www.axios.com/local/twin-cities/2021/03/01/minneapolis-triplex-legalize-impact-little, accessed September 25, 2022.

[135]. "St. Paul seeking ways to build more duplexes, triplexes, fourplexes," My Villager, July 21, 2021, https://myvillager.com/2021/07/21/st-paul-seeking-ways-to-build-more-duplexes-triplexes-fourplexes/, accessed September 25, 2022.

[136]. Afdhel Aziz, "How Boxabl Is Revolutionizing Affordable Housing With Its Unfolding House, And Customers Including Elon Musk Want In," Forbes, August 11, 2021, https://www.forbes.com/sites/afdhelaziz/2021/08/11/how-boxabl-is-revolutionizing-affordable-housing-with-its-unfolding-house-with-customers-like-elon-musk-and-1-billion-in-pre-orders/?sh=31777de67d78, accessed September 25, 2022.

[137]. "Manufactured Housing in the United Sttes," Manufactured Housing Institute, http://

www.manufacturedhousing.org/wp-content/uploads/2022/04/2022-MHI-Quick-Facts-updated-05-2022-2.pdf, accessed September 25, 2022.

[138]. "Impact," Local Initiatives Support Corporation, https://www.lisc.org/impact/, accessed September 25, 2022.

[139]. "Our Impact," Enterprise Community Partners, https://www.enterprisecommunity.org/about/our-impact, accessed September 25, 2022.

[140]. Karen Chapple, "Displacement: The misunderstood crisis," The Urban Institute, August 31, 2015, https://www.urban.org/urban-wire/displacement-misunderstood-crisis, accessed September 25, 2022.

[141]. Quoted in Roger Valdez, "Is Housing Displacement For New People, Jobs And Growth Really Happening?" Forbes, August 11, 2016, https://www.forbes.com/sites/rogervaldez/2016/08/11/is-housing-displacement-for-new-people-jobs-and-growth-really-happening/?sh=414338affed3, accessed September 25, 2022.

[142]. "About Taking Ownership PDX, LLC," Taking Ownership PDX, https://takingownershippdx.com/accessed September 25, 2022.

[143]. "The Anti-Displacement Tax Fund For Legacy Homeowners," Westside Future Fund, https://www.westsidefuturefund.org/homeonthewestside-adtfprogram/, accessed September 25, 2022.

[144]. Jacob Goldstein, "Why It's Illegal To Braid Hair Without A License," NPR, June 12, 2012, https://www.npr.org/sections/money/2012/06/21/154826233/why-its-illegal-to-braid-hair-without-a-license, accessed September 25, 2022.

[145]. Jacob Goldstein, "It's Now Legal to Braid Hair in Utah Without a License," NPR, August 9, 2012, https://www.npr.org/sections/money/2012/08/09/158498244/its-now-legal-to-braid-hair-in-utah-without-a-license, accessed September 25, 2022.